THE
CONDO OWNER'S
Answer Book

BETH A. GRIMM, ATTORNEY AT LAW

SPHINX® PUBLISHING
AN IMPRINT OF SOURCEBOOKS, INC.®
NAPERVILLE, ILLINOIS
www.SphinxLegal.com

First Edition, 2008

Published by: **Sphinx® Publishing, An Imprint of Sourcebooks, Inc.®**

Naperville Office
P.O. Box 4410
Naperville, Illinois 60567-4410
630-961-3900
Fax: 630-961-2168
www.sourcebooks.com
www.SphinxLegal.com

This publication is designed to provide accurate and authoritative information in regard
to the subject matter covered. It is sold with the understanding that the publisher is not
engaged in rendering legal, accounting, or other professional service. If legal advice or
other expert assistance is required, the services of a competent professional person
should be sought.
*From a Declaration of Principles Jointly Adopted by a Committee of the
American Bar Association and a Committee of Publishers and Associations*

This product is not a substitute for legal advice.
Disclaimer required by Texas statutes

Library of Congress Cataloging-in-Publication Data

Grimm, Beth A.
   The condo owner's answer book : the 250 most common questions about condominium
ownership / by Beth A. Grimm.
       p. cm.
   Includes index.
   ISBN 978-1-57248-633-1 (pbk. : alk. paper) 1. Condominiums--United States. 2.
Apartment houses, Cooperative--United States--Management. 3. Condominium associ-
ations--United States. I. Title.

HD7287.67.U5G75 2008
333.33'8--dc22
                                        2007043873

Printed and bound in the United States of America.
VP — 10 9 8 7 6 5 4 3 2 1

Dedication

Like my last book, this book is dedicated to *the selfless volunteer directors and committee members who step up to the plate in their homeowners' associations and give time and energy to running the ranch* in the face of challenging household and job responsibilities, a fast-moving and stressful world, and complaining owners, rising costs, threats of lawsuits, and other travesties, and who experience sleepless nights worrying about HOA business.

It is also dedicated *to the service provider volunteers in the CID industry* who contribute extra time to and treasure the noble cause of homeowner and board member education and work with like-minded contributors to brainstorm solutions to difficult problems. Those who do service and contribute their interests, hearts, and resources to bettering the community association industry stand out in the crowd of vendors, professionals, and others who merely offer services.

The book is also dedicated to *the many organizations and coalitions* dedicated to making the community association concept a working reality and to the leaders who start and run the organizations that educate, train, and help HOA boards, board members, managers, and homeowners.

And last, but certainly not least, this book is dedicated to the condo owners who pay attention to what is happening in their associations! Apathy is the number one cause of paralysis in homeowners' associations, which leads to the inability to exert beneficial change, and the number one reason why some boards are allowed to get out of control. Kudos to those who hunger for information and education. *This book was written for you!*

Contents

Foreword: How to Use This Book

You want to buy a condo, or you already have bought a condo and want to know more about what you bought, how things are supposed to work, and what your rights are. You are thinking about running for the board and want to know what it means to serve your association, or you are unhappy in your circumstances and want to know what you can do to remedy the situation. Maybe you just want to know more about condominiums in general.

This book is for anyone who wants to know more about condominium living. If you bought this book, you want answers, and you will find them here. This book will discuss things to watch out for in purchasing and owning a condominium, such as how to resolve issues, what problems might arise, and how the use of a condo might be restricted. This book will also give answers to common questions that are raised by people who are buying or who already own a condominium.

Purpose and Intent

Please do not take this resource book as an indication that condo living is either perfect on the one hand or fraught with problems on the other. There are millions of people living comfortably in their condos. Even though they are comfortable, however, many of these people probably wish they had really known what they were getting into before purchasing. Some owners might even be unhappy with their condos, their boards of directors, their association vendors, or their neighbors.

It is probably fair to say that most owners are quite happy with their purchases, that most associations are well run and successful, that the property is bound to appreciate in many areas of the country, and that in many cases condos are more affordable than single-family homes, offer more amenities, and present a very viable investment option.

And nothing beats a development that is well-kept, well-maintained, and well-operated for carefree living.

Substance

In this book you will find short, general explanations of relevant topics as well as questions, answers, and *Key Points*. The topics with the most universal appeal—or dare one say the most universally misunderstood subject matter—were chosen for this book. Some are sexier than others, but something is sure to strike a chord, especially if you are buying or selling condominiums as an investment or a job, are purchasing a condominium for yourself or a family member, already own a condominium, want to serve on the board or committee of a condominium, dislike your condominium association or board, have a complaint, hate your situation, or want out.

For this book, I have settled on the several basic categories within which the most common and universal questions seem to be asked. Since one chapter cannot cover any topic in full, when there are specific outside resources with more helpful information, those resources are discussed within that chapter. Finally, at the end of the book, there are comprehensive lists of resources that may have answers to questions that you will not find in this book.

Focus

Keep in mind the following important points about this book.

- This book is *not* meant to be a source of *legal advice* with regard to any scenario that seems the same or similar to the questions answered. The laws in different states vary considerably and one needs intimate knowledge of the laws in his or her state to be a good legal advisor. No single attorney can know the law in every state because on top of a particular state's law, there are the day-to-day experiences endemic to the geographical area and demographics of the people that factor into the equation. In addition, with regard to any particular dispute, there are often facts that, if not divulged to the advocate, would cloud his or her advice and might warrant a 180-degree turn in strategy.

• This book *is* meant to be a source of information that is not readily available. Even spending a lot of time searching on the Internet or at the library will not get you the kind of information that life experience brings. These are real-life questions and real-life answers that are provided by someone who, although a lawyer, does not believe litigation is necessary in most disputes, especially before exhausting all other avenues first. Each question has been asked by someone who has a problem for which there is a solution, and who would be helped by the breadth of questions and answers in this book.

• The perspective of the author is just one viewpoint, and seeking out additional information and suggestions via sources with other perspectives is always wise.

• The author of this book was born and raised in the Midwest, with strong ethical values, a fondness for the ownership of dirt, and a dislike of uncertainty and unreasonable and unethical behaviors.

• The author feels that with more information available, there will be fewer owners innocently roped into difficult living situations. Understanding what you are getting into with a condominium purchase is extremely important.

• The author also believes commendations should be given to the many volunteer leaders who serve their communities, especially in view of the fact that it can be a thankless job. Boards can become the recipients of criticism, scorn, and oftentimes unjustified distrust.

This book was written because of the author's strong desire to provide educational materials and helpful tools so that the public better understands what living in a condominium involves, what kinds of situations arise, how the situations can be addressed and resolved, and how condominium communities can thrive with the benefits of structure; actions of preventive law; and, orderly, pragmatic, and consensus-building practices.

I have the education and experience to be considered a credible resource. Although I am only one person, I have seen the condo world through many eyes. Besides being an attorney, mediator, and a speaker and author on many subjects, I own a condominium and have had some experience with the board in regard to tenant conduct when, on various occasions, my condo and tenants were chastised for violations of covenants that were actually occurring in the neighboring unit. As you can see, I have experienced condo issues firsthand, secondhand, thirdhand, and more.

The hardest part of putting together this kind of book is that there are so many questions, misconceptions, and misunderstandings. There are such mixed messages about the condominium style of living and what it entails. While the real estate section of your local newspaper advertises condo developments as the answer to affordable, carefree, *lock-and-go* living, the "Homes," "Living," or "Financial" sections might carry horror stories on the latest battle going on in your neighborhood over people, pets, and parking (commonly referred to as the "3Ps").

It is always important to keep a balanced perspective and to take the news stories with a grain of salt. Remember, sensationalism sells.

Use this book wisely and refer to it often. Watch for the *Key Points*. There are many scenarios in here that you may one day face, and you may find that taking preventive measures and educating yourself will result in much less grief. My motto is, "For every problem, there is a solution." The constant challenge is finding the right solution.

Introduction

The homeowners' association (HOA) industry involving condominiums, shared-amenity living, and shared responsibility is full of misconceptions derived from negative reports and portrayals in newspapers, magazines, tabloids, and even on television and in the movies. The tabloids love a good "the board president was run over ten times by a resident who was not allowed to wash his car in the common area" story. The television series *X-Files* presented an episode based on a situation in which the board eliminated—yes, I mean that literally—owners who did not follow the rules. And when Jerry Seinfeld's father became the subject of a nasty recall battle because he was suspected of pilfering association money when seen driving around in a new Cadillac purchased for him by his son, the audiences loved it.

So, are there answers to the questions and quandaries that arise? Yes, there are. And many can be found in this book or in the resources identified within. If you are seeking answers to questions and ways to work out or find solutions, you are in the right place. If you want to pay a lawyer to front your complaint and shield you from a logical and cost-effective solution, go to the Yellow Pages and prepare to be shocked. The costs of litigation are out of sight for the average person. And although lawyers and judges are highly trained and generally experienced individuals, not many (of the thousands with the degree or title) have the range of options available to resolve condo-related issues. Escalating differences of opinion can lead to making a mountain out of a molehill. Using a lawyer who does not provide a full gamut of options and does not know the area of law in his or her state related to condominiums *can* hurt you, as can ending up before a judge that has not had experience with cases in this form of real estate, no matter which side of the table you are sitting on.

Litigation should be a last resort to solving problems and differences of opinion, while looking for answers should be the first. You, are in the right place.

Chapter 1

BUYER BEWARE— OR AT LEAST BE SMART!

- If I am considering buying a condo, what can I do to make sure I do not get scammed?
- What is the first step in deciding if I want to consider buying a condo?
- How would I decide if purchasing either a condominium or an attached house where a homeowners' association is involved is a better choice for me than a single-family residence with no such association?
- What are the differences in what I should look for if I am purchasing a condo for use as my primary residence and if I am purchasing a condo to be used as a rental or investment property?
- Can the rules or regulatory documents of an association restrict certain people from purchasing a condominium or residing in what they purchase?
- What do I need to do before I sign the contract? Do I need a lawyer or is this the kind of thing I can do completely on my own?
- Are there any tax issues to be concerned with when purchasing a condo as opposed to another type of property, either as a primary residence or an investment property?
- What is the expense of insurance?
- How are property taxes handled?
- Once I decide a condominium is right for me, what are the most important questions to ask when shopping for a condo? How do I find the right condo?
- How can I avoid getting into a difficult practical situation when purchasing a condo?
- How can I avoid getting into a difficult financial situation when purchasing a condo?
- How can I obtain information I need from an association if the association is not willing to give it to me?
- I am looking in three different condo developments and want to compare notes—what are some of the red flags that I should watch out for?
- Where can I find important information about an association?
- My association just took over from the developer and discovered that the budget was extremely inadequate. What do we do?

If I am considering buying a condo, what can I do to make sure I do not get scammed?

Here is what *not* to do: do *not* trust yourself (if you do *not* have a working knowledge of homeowners' associations); do *not* trust a real estate agent who does not sell very many condos; and, do *not* think it does not matter who you talk to.

What is the first step in deciding if I want to consider buying a condo?

The first step is to think very hard about what you want in a living situation. Educate yourself on what a condominium is. Understand that you would be purchasing a home that is similar in many ways to an apartment, but without the easy out that a lease gives you. Understand that you cannot choose or control your neighbors. You have to hope for reasonable people who can coexist in a densely populated development. On the other hand, consider your financial capability and whether a condominium is the only affordable option. Ask yourself if having a pool, spa, park, business center, fitness room, clubhouse, or other amenity is important to you (understanding that you will have to pay for the amenity whether you use it or not). Consider that having the extra layer of governance could be an advantage in keeping the development together.

Talk to friends who live in condos. See what they think and whether they enjoy their situations. Almost everyone knows someone who has had "condo experience" of some kind. Do not get your information from the newspapers. Understand that the information printed there has one purpose only—to sell newspapers. And understand that the vocal minority—often those who complain the loudest—are not the purveyors of the most balanced information.

How would I decide if purchasing either a condominium or an attached house where a homeowners' association is involved is a better choice for me than a single-family residence with no such association?

The answer to this question depends on the reasons you might consider a condominium. Is affordability an issue? Condominiums are often priced lower than single-family homes in the same geographic area. Are you looking to purchase in an area that has more condominiums than single-family residences, such as Orange County, California? In some cases, it is hard to find single-family residential properties that are not connected to homeowners' associations.

Are you interested in the *lock and go* capability of a condo? It often feels safer to lock the doors and leave your house if it is in an area where your neighbors are close and someone is always out and about, making it less obvious that the owner is on vacation. If you know your neighbors, they can keep watch over your place for you. Is the idea that someone else maintains the property enticing? Some people do not like to work in the yard or on the buildings, while others do not like having the responsibility of finding contractors to do the necessary work.

There are considerations related to financing a condominium that may be important. Can you qualify under the lender's criteria for the mortgage payment *and* the monthly assessment payment that is required for a condominium? Are you willing to risk that the assessment may be increased, irrespective of your ability to pay?

What are the differences in what I should look for if I am purchasing a condo for use as my primary residence and if I am purchasing a condo to be used as a rental or investment property?

Some of the things to consider are as follows.

- Make sure to find out whether the governing documents limit leasing. Some associations have restrictions on leasing your unit within the first year or two of purchase. Some restrict the total number of units in the building that can be leased out at one time. Some associations prohibit leasing altogether, while others allow temporary exceptions for hardship and special circumstances.

- Find out whether there are likely to be noise issues. Sometimes you can get into a really uncomfortable position if you place tenants in a close, dense living situation and either they or their neighbors are inconsiderate people. If you do not protect yourself with a lease that allows you to evict tenants who cause trouble in the association, you may be caught in a difficult situation where the tenants are the ones actually violating the rules but you get stuck paying the fines.

- Condos tend to make good rental properties from the standpoint that you do not have to arrange for building repairs (except within the unit), lawn mowing, snow shoveling, etc. This type of work is done for you through the association (but, remember that you pay the cost as part of your association fees).

Can the rules or regulatory documents of an association restrict certain people from purchasing a condominium or residing in what they purchase?

The answer is yes. There are legal *age-restricted* communities. But even in those cases the problem is not in purchasing the property, but rather in placing a resident in the unit. In most age-restricted communities there are bans on residents who are younger than 55 years of age, while in some communities residents under the age of 62 are not allowed because of the way the federal law is written.

There are exceptions for caregivers, disabled adult children, and a few others, but these developments are basically for seniors only.

Interestingly enough, there was a news story a few years ago on an association in Florida that banned lawyers (what a concept!). Associations may not discriminate against owners in the purchase and sale of any condominium—to the extent the association gets involved in the purchase and sale, which would be more in a *cooperative* than in a condominium—on any grounds that could be considered discrimination or in violation of the federal or particular state Constitution.

This means that if you want to purchase a condominium in an association and for reasons other than the community being a valid age-restricted community you are told that you cannot, this may be unlawful discrimination and you should see a lawyer. There are many documents that exist in the United States that ban certain people—based on race or religion or the like—that are simply unenforceable and illegal.

What do I need to do before I sign the contract? Do I need a lawyer or is this the kind of thing I can do completely on my own?

It is easy for a lawyer to advise you to get an attorney. All contracts have ramifications and buying a condo is a big deal for most people, as it is possibly their single most expensive investment to date. Keep in mind, however, when seeking advice on the purchase of a condominium, that a lawyer who knows condominium law may not be as well-versed in the law of the purchase and sale of real property and vice versa. You should understand that signing a contract has legal ramifications and if you go forward in any real estate transaction without legal assistance there are considerable risks. In regard to a condo purchase, it is good to know what you are getting into, and a lawyer will be able to explain that to you.

As with any real property purchase, the buy-sell process of a condominium involves an offer, acceptance, inspections, contingencies, etc. It gets more complicated when inspections indicate the need for repairs because there may be a question as to whether the association or the owner is responsible for the cost. Termite inspections are famous for uncovering problems that need to be addressed to satisfy lenders, while the association may prefer to make the repair on a different timeline. If a condo needs a new roof before a lender will fund a loan but the association cannot afford one or prefers to defer the replacement for a year, it can cause problems.

> **Key Point**
>
> Take noise nuisance disclosures seriously. These tend to come up in conversion condos and poorly built buildings that lack insulation, solid flooring, and double walls between the units. Excessive noise transmission can ruin your life, and you cannot always fix it.

Occupancy ratios and litigation are subjects that may affect your ability to get a loan and close the transaction. They do not arise until well into the lender application process. This is different than in a single-family home situation. It generally matters if the association has a high ratio of nonresident owners to resident owners. (The lending pool is limited for developments that have more than 50% nonresident owners.)

The most important thing of all to understand, though, is that if you are not well-versed in what condominium living and the governing documents and rules are all about, you better work with trusted vendors who are. If you go in blind you may end up with the surprise of your life, be it good or bad.

Are there any tax issues to be concerned with when purchasing a condo as opposed to another type of property, either as a primary residence or an investment property?

The answer is yes, there are tax issues to be concerned with, but the tax issues do not differ greatly from any that come up in transactions involving other types of real property purchases. In other words, whether you are dealing with property transfers and the resultant basis issues, divorce settlements, gifted property, death, or 1031 exchanges, tax issues can arise. More answers for specific tax-related questions can be found in tax-related publications or in discussions with your accountant.

What is the expense of insurance?
You may be asking what kind of insurance the association needs to carry and whether you will need to purchase individual insurance for your condo. In most cases, the homeowners' association pays for a master policy for the building with coverage for normal hazards like fire and other casualties. In areas prone to hurricanes, tornadoes, or earthquakes, the insurance availability and cost can depend on the level of risk perceived at any given time. In other words, an association often ends up at the mercy of the insurance carriers. Keep in mind, however, that this may also be the case if you were to purchase a single-family home. However, condominium associations are treated as commercial entities for purposes of purchasing insurance, which can mean higher rates per square foot than for single-family homes.

Generally, the homeowners' association pays for the master building insurance coverage out of the assessments that are collected. However, as an owner in such a community, you must purchase your own coverage for accidents within your unit and any personal property. The most common policy for owners in condominiums is referred to as an *HO-6*.

How are property taxes handled?

Usually each owner of a unit pays property taxes on his or her own unit. Generally, the common-area property is not taxed. However, there have been cases in which some localities have sought to tax common areas. Whether or not your locality is one that does this is something you can find out by either calling your local tax assessor or asking the association.

Once I decide a condominium is right for me, what are the most important questions to ask when shopping for a condo? How do I find the right condo?

First, you need to locate your area or areas of choice.

Find a Realtor who is an area specialist and commonly deals with condominiums. Getting referrals from satisfied clients is the best way to find an honest, reliable real estate agent.

Be sure to drive through the complexes that interest you, look around, check out the condition of the buildings as well as the common areas like the pool, clubhouse, greenbelt, parks, etc. Are the neighborhoods well-tended and well-kept? Are the common areas clean and well-kept? Are the streets and driveways fairly clear of distracting vehicles, or is every inch of street running through the development cluttered with parked vehicles, leaving only a narrow thoroughfare? Is the landscaping kept up? Are the trees trimmed? Are the trees very large and close to fences or homes? Are there sidewalks? Does the neighborhood look kid-friendly (if you have kids) or quiet (if you do not)? Are the balconies cluttered with items that should be in storage?

Try to drive through during the day so you can see the condition of the complex, the fences, yards, and buildings, and also drive through in the evening so you can see what happens when everyone comes home from work. Do the people you see wave and smile? What is around the development—shops or open space? Are people out walking around, or does the development look deserted? Are the mailboxes overflowing with advertisements, or are they neat and tidy?

You know more about what you like than your real estate agent does. Some places you can scope out yourself, but others, like a gated community, might require forming a relationship with a real estate agent. The important thing to ask is whether you can see yourself living there.

How do I avoid getting into a difficult practical situation when purchasing a condo? I own a minivan, and after I moved into my townhouse I discovered that it barely fits in the garage. Everyone else must have the same problem getting in and out of their cars in the cramped garages, because the streets in this new development are overrun with cars. It looks like a parking lot. Is there anything I can do?

This is one of those very difficult situations and it illustrates how a dream can quickly turn into a nightmare if you do not pay attention to detail. Many developments look a lot different in the early phases when the properties are just built because everything is brand new, neat, and tidy, and hardly anyone lives there yet. Things look perfect, and people forget the community will not always look that way. Once the entire development is finished being built, the beautiful view from the model homes might no longer exist. The streets, although beautiful and free of cars at the beginning, might later be cluttered with vehicles, especially if they are public streets.

On the one hand, the association may not decide to adopt rules about street parking because of potential issues. If you like the streets free of parked vehicles, this could backfire on you. On the other hand, the association may decide to set rules prohibiting street parking, which would present a problem for you if you were, for example, counting on parking your third or fourth vehicle on the street. These are questions you may want to attempt to clarify before you sign on the dotted line.

> ## Key Point
> Do a drive through and look around—day, afternoon, and night! Take off your blinders and give the place a real, responsible, and truthful assessment. Take along a friend or family member for the sake of objectivity.

What you have to do is envision what conditions might be like after every single unit is sold. It seldom happens that everyone is outside at one time, but if even 20% of the residents are outside at any given time, in most developments it will seem like a lot more people than you expected. Most people work during the day, but on weekends, if the weather is nice, people come outside and bring their children, pets, and visitors with them. Try to imagine what it would be like if you were having a family gathering or a party. Consider what it would mean to your neighbors (how close are they?) and what it would mean to your guests (is there enough guest parking?). Try to imagine how you would be affected if your neighbors had a party.

In the scenario about the small garage space, anyone could have missed the fact that the garages were constructed so that no one with a minivan would be able to easily get the vehicle into the garage without a lot of consternation. However, in that case, the fact that there are over 1,200 units in the development that all have narrow tandem garages stacked on top of each other as close as possible should present a clue that parking your family vehicle might be an issue.

When you drive through a development and see that the street entryways to a line of garages are narrow—say, fifteen to twenty feet—and the garages are just barely at or over the width of your normal-size family vehicle, you can imagine what occurs when all the garbage cans are out for pickup on any given day. It is nearly impossible to get your vehicle in and out of the area, let alone the garages. If your neighbors all leave for work at the same time, there could be a traffic jam in the garage area. Make sure that when you drive through a development, you pay attention to these kinds of details. Driving through a development and checking to see what color the units are, what people have on their patios and decks, and how the grounds are maintained is not enough.

> ### Key Point
>
> If you drive a Hummer or any other gigantic vehicle, understand that you may have to park a half mile down the road.

How do I avoid getting into a difficult financial situation when purchasing a condo? I just moved into my condo—new to me but about 20 years old—and I am hearing rumors that the whole development needs to get new plumbing. I have been told that there will be a special assessment of $6,000 per unit, and even worse, that I will have to move out for at least six weeks! I just got unpacked. Needless to say, I am not happy. How could I have found out about this before I purchased my new home?

Since there will be more information on assessments in a later chapter, this question will be answered here from the standpoint of what it is you might do to avoid finding yourself in this type of situation in the future.

Before you sign your purchase contract, you should hire a building inspector to inspect any property you are considering buying. However, you may find that in a condominium setting your inspector cannot get access to all the areas he or she needs in order to accurately assess the condition of the *common systems*. The *common systems* are the buildings, walls (exterior and those between the units), roofs, pipes, wires, conduit, decks, patios, walkways, and portions of the components outside the unit. Potential purchasers in a condominium are often told that there is no need or that they have no right to inspect common areas because the association takes care of them.

However, here is where you have to be careful—do not assume that everything will be taken care of by the association. The association does not always take care of everything that owners expect it will.

This means that you should push to have your inspector check out everything that he or she can. Encourage the inspector to point out things that need an explanation.

You can and should hire a pest inspector for any real estate purchase that involves a residential or commercial building. However, again, you may find that in the condominium setting, your inspector cannot get access to all the areas he or she needs in order to accurately assess the condition of the building, decks, and walkways around your home in regard to termites or dry rot. And again, potential purchasers in a condominium are often told that there is no need to inspect certain areas because the association will take care of them. Again, though, owners are often disappointed by what the association ends up doing or not doing. Too often a homeowner's expectations are not completely met, which usually comes from a lack of education and experience on either one side or both sides of the table.

How can I obtain information I need from an association if the association is not willing to give it to me?

This question presents another difficult situation. Why do potential buyers sometimes not receive the information they request?

You might not have received copies of the documents you requested because it is not convenient for the association to give them to you. It could be because the association is not required to give them to you by law.

You can ask the seller for copies of the documents, but neither the board nor the management company for any association wants to do extra work or unwittingly establish a legal relationship with an outside party, which can lead to it being sued. Outsiders are not generally entitled to private information about the association. If the seller asks for a set of documents from the association, there is likely to be a charge that you would have to pay.

The recorded regulatory documents can be obtained by going or writing to the local county recorder's office, but again, there will be a charge for the documents. Realtors, title companies, and others can get public documents of associations and sometimes even additional information from a site called CondoCerts at **www.condocerts.com**, where associations can choose to register their information.

Probably more often than not, however, as a potential buyer who wants a lot of information about a particular condominium, you will run into difficulties getting it until you are under a contract to purchase. Once under contract, you can make requests of the seller to obtain the information for you, and he or she should be able to get most of it.

There are disclosure laws and rights to retrieve association documents in most states. A prospective purchaser is often barred from association meetings. However, you could ask the seller if you could attend a meeting with him or her, and sometimes the board will let you in. If the board does not take attendance, you can probably get in on your own (although that would show that you have a board that is not very diligent, if the members do not know who is attending board meetings).

If you can get into a development and talk to owners in the development, you may be able to gather some useful information. However, while this is a way to seek information in any residential neighborhood, the accuracy of the information may be questionable. Some people might be happy in a neighborhood, while others in the same neighborhood are dissatisfied. Also, sometimes personal grudges lead to the dissemination of misleading and unfairly biased information. If you happen to stop an owner who is very dissatisfied with the board because he or she just got a notice that his or her dilapidated Jeep can no longer be parked in his or her driveway, you are probably not going to hear a glowing report about living in the association.

This is why the best advice may be to work with an area specialist when you are looking for your condo. A real estate agent who has previously sold homes in any particular condominium development probably knows if there are any issues that came up for his or her buyers after purchase. He or she probably has information that you will never be able to get ahold of on your own, and also may be more frank than a developer's sales representative in a new development.

In any case, it is important to obtain the most current set of restrictions because they may have been amended by the membership at some point after the development was built. In many states, the statutes change, which means that associations need to amend their regulatory documents so they can act properly under the law.

It is not so easy to get association documents and sometimes not easy to get someone to talk to you at all. Some potential purchaser or Realtor inquiries are met with scorn—a "why bother me until you live here" sort of mentality. However, if you are persistent, the owner/seller of the development is generally entitled to have copies of records from the association, and the law generally requires that the owner/seller be provided with financial information and budgets for the association. This means that if an owner is motivated to sell, he or she might provide the information. However, the same legal premise that guides managers and boards applies to owners—i.e., without a potential purchaser under a purchase agreement, no owner is required to provide this information.

No one is required to give any information to a real estate agent, either. However, if a seller wants to be helpful, he or she can usually get information on most issues that a potential purchaser wants to know about. In some communities, the management company and real estate agent work together to make information available so that potential buyers are not placed in a position in which they need to make an offer on a property just to find out sufficient information that they would need to know in order to feel comfortable making a purchase offer.

If you can get the last financial statement showing actual income and expenses—having financial statements on hand from the last two years is even better—and the prior year's and current year's budget for the association, you can begin to get a picture of the association's finances. Hopefully, these documents will show actual projections for certain expenses and will allow you to compare one year with another, but there are still certain things to look for even if they do not show actual projections, like how much money the association has in its reserves. You may have to ask the seller for this financial information, because in most jurisdictions neither the management company nor the board is anxious or willing to hand out private information about the association. In most states, owners are entitled to ask for this kind of financial information if they do not have it, and in many cases it is provided on an annual basis.

I am looking in three different condo developments and want to compare notes—what are some of the red flags that I should watch out for?

There are four things that you should do.

1. Look at the operating costs of the association.
2. Find out how much money is in the association reserves.
3. Read the fine print.
4. Go over all the governing and regulatory documents of the association.

First, in comparing projected expenses with actual costs, you can look for operating costs in certain areas that might indicate a red flag. Watch for extraordinary costs in the areas of plumbing repairs, electrical repairs, water damage repairs, and the like. These can be red flags that indicate you should ask more questions.

Example: If an association projected $5,000 for plumbing repairs in a given year, perhaps for slab leaks or common-area plumbing, and the expenses for that year were $25,000, that would indicate the probability that there is some bigger problem with the plumbing. It could be a fluke, such as one project gone terribly wrong. However, more likely, it means that the board will eventually find out that there is something wrong with the plumbing in all the units, especially if the building is old. Even when the board of directors *does* figure this out right away, the expenses can mount exponentially. If the pipes in a condominium development are beginning to leak in the slabs or in the walls, the association will constantly be hit with demands from owners to repair paint, flooring, and possibly personal property that is damaged by the water intruding into the unit from the leaky pipes. So, the $25,000 might be for plumbing repairs, or it might be for costs related to the leak. It might be for leak detection costs, or for mold that had to be mediated because of a water leak.

The difference in comparison between the low-budget projection and the exorbitant expense would be a red flag, whether it was in the category of plumbing, electrical, roof maintenance and repairs, or another area that involved a common system that might have to be replaced if worn out. It might relate to an outdated boiler system in a high-rise, for example, where the board is still estimating expenses based on maintenance costs that were realistic ten or twenty years ago, but not now. It might be that the boiler is not even replaceable with a like product, and the expense of changing systems is beyond anyone's expectations. An unanticipated or unbudgeted sizable expense might be an indicator of faulty wiring or a roof that is failing, or even paint that looks good, but is no longer providing water-proofing protection for the

> ### Key Point
> Inadequate concentration and expertise in regard to an association's budgeting could spell disaster for owners.

siding of the units. It also might just be gross inadequacy in the planning for the association expenses—those working on the budget are often volunteers that have no special expertise with building systems, and if they have not hired the right kind of experts to help with the budget planning, it could be disastrous for owners.

Second, compare the association reserves with the current level of funding. In a condominium, since all owners share the costs of maintaining the buildings and systems, the board should be collecting money to put away to maintain, repair, and replace the components as they need attention. The board should be reporting on the funds that are set aside for this purpose. In most states there are at least some requirements related to reserves, and some governing documents have specific requirements. Several states have very detailed statutes about reserves. For example, California has a very specific disclosure requirement, which includes a study requirement that involves periodic inspections and projections about funds that will be needed in the coming years; comparisons between the amount of money in the reserve accounts and the amount of money the studies project will be needed in order to fully fund future maintenance expenses; and, if there are shortfalls in the percentage funded, figuring out how the difference will be raised, such as with anticipated special assessments or bank loans. The disclosure needs to show per unit projections.

Reserve disclosure requirements are common, but the requirement to fully fund reserves is not. Thus, when considering purchasing a unit in a condominium project, you will want to obtain whatever reports exist showing the plan for funding major repairs and replacements. Roofs, siding, and painting are common major projects, and associations struggle to have enough money when it comes time for these major repairs and replacements to be done. It is not uncommon for people to find dry rot, siding damage, or termite issues, any of which can increase the cost of the reparation work, and therefore, it is not uncommon to underestimate the cost of the entire job if you do not take into account these kinds of problems that may not be obvious to the naked eye. Therefore, if the paperwork that you receive indicates a major repair is coming soon, it could also mean a *special assessment* will be necessary as well. Ask questions about the upcoming repair if the information you receive is not clear. Your questions should be directed to the seller, who should be able to get answers even if you cannot get them from the real estate agent, manager, or association.

> ## Key Point
>
> Watch for hidden indicators in the "comments" of the financial documents. They will all contain a certain amount of "CYA" statements. Professionals tend to include several comments needed to avoid being sued.

Third, you need to read the fine print. The reserve study preparers and CPAs usually make several disclaimers in the reports they provide. It is important to read these financial reports closely. It is not a good sign if there are no reserves records available. If there are, but the records show no reserves money in the bank, that is not a good sign either—unless you prefer to "pay as you go" for everything.

Compare the Governing Documents

Finally, you should look at the governing and regulatory documents to find out who fixes what. If the documents are unclear, then you should ask questions. Do not expect the condominium association to fix everything for just the assessment cost. In some associations, owners are responsible for maintaining and replacing windows, doors, utility closets, air conditioners, heaters, and hot water heaters. In others, the board is responsible for these repairs. Sometimes, owners share water costs, and there are not separate meters. In other cases, everyone pays for his or her own water. (You might think that you would prefer having your water paid in the assessment, but if your neighbors use twice as much as you, you would be paying part of their costs when water is shared. People tend to conserve more when they are paying their own water bills.) Look for sections in the governing documents on maintenance, assessments, and uses. If you cannot find them, it probably means the provisions are buried somewhere rather than segregated, and you might even need a lawyer to help you dissect the legal documents.

Where can I find important information about an association?

You do not necessarily need a lawyer to recognize problems in an association. Sometimes obvious issues show up in the minutes of a homeowners' association meeting. In most, if not all, states, owners have the right to obtain copies of an association meetings' minutes— both board meetings and membership meetings. A buyer may ask for copies of the meetings' minutes from the seller. Realtors are starting to add the last twelve months of minutes to their escrow demands, as minutes can be very telling about an association. Remember, however, that as a buyer you cannot go directly to the association for minutes—they are not public records. Visit **www.condocerts.com** to see if the association you are considering posts its minutes on the website.

What is so enlightening about minutes? One can tell from minutes whether:

> **Key Point**
> Minutes often provide the juiciest gossip and information about what goes on in a homeowners' association.

- the board is organized and businesslike;
- the secretary knows what he or she is doing in regard to the minutes;
- the board and association tend to be gossipy;
- the board or minute-taker has recently defamed anyone; or,
- the association is plagued with any kinds of problems, including architectural violations, contractor mistakes, individual owner complaints, broken sprinklers, roof leaks, and insurance claims.

Generally, the minutes should reflect who is present and whether there is a quorum; provide reports of committees and officers; reveal financial reporting by the treasurer; and, disclose old business, new business, and the motions made, along with whether they passed. However, some minute-takers get carried away and the minutes end up looking like a gossipy newsletter. Sometimes there is a long list of business items related to repairs, complaints, or other problems. The most common request for minutes, if one is made, is for a year's worth. Sometimes a board does not meet very often, but if there are gaps in sequence in the minutes, or there are no minutes available to obtain, it is a sign that the association may not be well-organized.

My association just took over from the developer and discovered that the budget was extremely inadequate. What do we do?

There are some cases where the developer of the properties *lowballs* assessments. What does this mean? To market the properties, the developer has an interest in keeping the assessments as low as possible. Assessments are factored into the consideration of how much a purchaser can qualify for when applying for a loan. In other words, the assessment is added to the mortgage payment when the lender is considering the debt-to-loan ratio.

Therefore, it makes sense that the lower the assessment, the more people there will be who can qualify to buy a condominium in the development. Sometimes developers subsidize the costs of operations to help keep the assessments low. One example is if the developer pays for watering the lawns and green spaces to keep things looking nice during the selling period. When the developer sells out and the homeowners' association takes over, the costs go up because then the homeowners are paying the cost to water the lawns and green spaces.

There are other causes of this lowballing effect. Some states' Departments of Real Estate sample budgets are too low and underestimate the costs of maintenance. When it comes time to make repairs based on the budget prepared for approval by the Department of Real Estate, the homeowners' association finds out that the costs are higher than anticipated.

> **Key Point**
>
> Developer lowballing is a problem, whether intentional or not. It can take owners by surprise, and leave associations without enough reserves.

Developer lowballing takes many owners by surprise. Many purchasers obtain condominiums—and other properties, as well, for that matter—by stretching what they have available to spend, making sacrifices, or counting on an upcoming raise. Many are able to purchase a condominium only by the skin of their teeth, and when the assessment starts to go up, they find themselves in financial trouble.

Condominiums are commonly marketed as a carefree living product whereby you simply pay an assessment each month that covers all or most of the costs of living there. However, this is not usually the truth.

Still, even if the condominium falls short of some of the criteria mentioned in this chapter, you may have found the perfect property for you. It may be overpriced, in an area you would not normally choose, underfunded in reserves, densely populated, and contain many other negatives, but if it has just the view you want, a pool, or other amenities; is a limited commodity of some kind (such as a marina property); is convenient to work or school; or, is the vacation home you always dreamed of, you may decide to throw caution to the wind and buy something that, albeit not perfect, serves you well or proves to be a viable real estate investment.

Chapter 2

UNDERSTANDING WHAT YOU BOUGHT

- Did I just mortgage myself for thirty years for airspace?
- I signed some papers in escrow, but they were too long to read and in legal jargon. What did I get myself into?
- What more do I need to know about a homeowners' association?
- Since I am "king or queen of my castle," nobody can tell me what to do in my condominium, right?

Did I just mortgage myself for thirty years for airspace?

While the purchase of *airspace* is a difficult concept to grasp because of a long history in the United States of pride in land ownership, it is usually what you get when purchasing a condominium. However, the airspace is yours to decorate, come home to, and call your own. But do not be fooled—there is a lot more to learn about what you can and cannot do in your own home when it is a condo.

I signed some papers in escrow, but they were too long to read and in legal jargon. What did I get myself into?

The papers in any real estate transaction are daunting, but they are especially confusing in a condominium purchase. On top of the usual paperwork, there are also governing documents for the association—the Association Articles of Incorporation, Bylaws, and the Declaration of Restrictions (commonly called CC&Rs—covenants, conditions, and restrictions). You also have the budget, the financials, and the most recent reserve study. There is no reasonable way to digest all of this information as you are signing to verify that you received these papers! The following paragraphs will give you, in a nutshell, the basic outline of what you bought.

When one purchases a condominium, he or she is essentially purchasing airspace plus some property owned in common with strangers. A purchaser might also get a garage, parking space, deck, or some additional component, but basically there is a singular-plus-a-shared ownership scheme. The actual thing that is purchased is described in the document filled with the legal jargon.

Most often the box that the owner actually owns alone is called a *separate interest* or something similar—a unit, co-op, dwelling, residence, apartment, or other word symbolizing the space in which the person is to reside. In a commercial condominium, it would be the space in which the person would work. The rest of the building or structure that houses this space is usually owned in common with the other condominium owners in the same development or complex. Sometimes the shared part of the ownership is one building, and sometimes it includes all the buildings in the development.

Simply put, the document that is recorded on the property purchased—which commonly includes a separate interest (yours) coupled with a common interest of some kind (the portion that is owned with the neighbors)—contains restrictions on the way the property may be used, which are most often recorded by the original owner of the land. In dividing the land into two or more plots, the developer plans the project and then writes restrictions on the use of the property to keep the development operating and looking similar to the way it was originally set up. Two or more owners who were not the original developers can also agree to these kinds of use restrictions for their adjacent plots of land. In fact, sometimes an owner of a large home will divide the home and sell off sections of it as condominiums.

Once these restrictions are properly recorded, they attach themselves to the land and stay there, even when the land is bought and sold. The restrictions can be changed or terminated only if a sufficient number of affected owners agree, according to the amendment clause found in the regulatory document.

The *recorded document* may be called a Declaration of Restrictions; Deed Restrictions; Declaration Establishing a Condominium; Condominium Regime; Declaration of Covenants, Conditions, and Restrictions (CC&Rs); regulatory documents; or, a similar name. The recorded document is the regulatory document for the properties within the development. These documents provide rights and obligations related to the properties that are supposed to be enforced and applied consistently among owners and the interests in property encompassed. For ease of understanding, this book will use the terms *declaration* or *Declaration of Restrictions* interchangeably to mean any of the documents previously listed.

> **Key Point**
>
> Officially recorded restrictions on condominium property stick like crazy glue. You agree to them simply by purchasing the property. You do not have to verbally agree or sign a written statement to become subject to them.

When a person buys a condominium or piece of property with regulatory restrictions on it, the person is considered to have legally consented and agreed to accept the regulatory documents. And when there is a homeowners' association, the new owners commonly become part of it, often whether they want to or not. Some associations provide for voluntary membership in the association, but for the most part, membership is mandatory. One cannot claim ignorance to avoid the restrictions. Anyone who purchases a condominium—or any other piece of property, for that matter—is said to have what is called *constructive legal notice* of any regulations that attach to the property by virtue of the fact that the regulatory document is a recorded document that will show up in a title search if the sale is above-board and the title search is done properly.

Besides this *real property* aspect—bringing condominiums under the realm of real property law—there is also the *contractual* aspect of the relationship between a condo owner and an association, which brings the Declaration of Restrictions under the realm of contract law. If the declaration is under contract law, then contract principles may also apply to the owner.

A person is deemed to have agreed to the contract to be a part of the association simply by purchasing property in the development. No one can *unilaterally* (without the participation of other parties owning property in the same development) lawfully change the real property regulations or the contract embodied in a Declaration of Restrictions that is recorded against a condominium property. It takes the consent of all the parties, or the percentage specified by the declaration, or a new law or case decision that overrides the document, to change it.

At least you own your own box filled with airspace, and you probably think that means that you can do anything you want to do in that confined space. Unfortunately, you cannot. You can paint, decorate, lounge, watch

> ### Key Point
> An owner of a condominium becomes a party to a contract with a lot of legalese in it that more or less takes an interpreter to explain.

television, eat, sleep, and enjoy your condo unit, but you are required to be cognizant of your neighbors' rights to enjoy their boxes of airspace as well. You cannot conduct yourself as if you live in a soundproof, smell-proof vacuum. You may be prohibited from holding personal workout sessions in your living room, inviting over your chanting buddies, holding choir practice, or smoking cigarettes in your own home.

You cannot start knocking down walls, raising the ceiling, putting in skylights, or adding a bathroom without regard for your neighbors or the structure itself. You must pay attention to the rights of the board—and in many jurisdictions, the corresponding rights of your neighbors—to enforce the restrictions on the property. You may not be able to have the pet you want, the Hummer you want (especially if it will not fit into a parking space or garage), or the colorful window treatments you so dearly love. You may be restricted in the number or types of signs, banners, potted plants, and knickknacks that you are allowed to have on your front porch, patio, or balcony. You may not be able to move in all your cousins and uncles, run your business in your home, or practice your scream therapy. (See more on this in Chapter 7.)

What more do I need to know about a homeowners' association? I moved in less than a week ago and already had a visit from my local,"friendly" welcome wagon representative who said a lot more than "welcome to the neighborhood." She "forgot" to bring coupons for discounts from local businesses, freshly baked cookies, emergency numbers, the HOA contact information, a directory of neighbors, a list of events coming up, or anything meaningful to me. What she did bring is a list of rules for me to read. So much for a warm and fuzzy welcome.

Unfortunately, this type of "welcome" is not really surprising, and it is obviously not the way to make people who have just moved in feel welcome. One of the major problems many associations face is a lack of training in communications on the part of those in charge. More often than not, there is no welcome wagon visit at all—and maybe that is better than a welcome wagon visit such as the one described. Top that off with a failure on the part of the board to properly instruct committees and advise those serving the association, and you have the potential for problems.

> **Key Point**
>
> Welcoming newcomers to the neighborhood by passing out the rules without using common courtesies may lead to the grooming of a combatant.

Since I am "king or queen of my castle," nobody can tell me what to do in my condominium, right?

Not exactly. All property owners are subject to some limits on their land. The closer the density of the property, the more rules one will normally see. It is part of living in society. And keep in mind there would be no need for rules if there were not people who disregarded them. The number of rules a community adopts often has a direct correlation to the number of problems in the development.

People who bristle at the thought of having their lives controlled by the landlords of the world probably would not be happy in a condominium association where many of the rules are similar to those in an apartment building. In fact, people may be much more unhappy when they find themselves living in a condominium they own that has the same rules as their last apartment.

While owners might love the tax write-offs they get with property ownership, if they run into problems—for example, making enemies with the neighbors—they could find themselves unable to relocate because of the money they have tied up in the condo. When people do not understand what they are getting into before these types of problems arise, they can end up making their own lives miserable along with the lives of those around them.

Being able to say, "I am a homeowner," may be part of the American dream, but if you are a condo owner, you are not always "king or queen of your castle." If your neighbors start to close in on you, or the associations' budget stretches your ability to pay assessments, this dream could turn into a nightmare for you. You are not solely in charge of your investment when you purchase a condominium. The management of the building or complex is put into the hands of volunteers. If the volunteers are wise and reasonable people, or have the wherewithal to hire wise and reasonable professionals and honest vendors, then things will probably be fine. On the other hand, if the association is poorly run, your investment may be at risk.

People tend to overlook these kinds of limitations when deciding to buy a condominium. In many cases, it is the look or layout of the place and amenities like a pool, park, or courtyard that appeal to buyers. But the other side of the coin is that the same rules that keep the complex looking nice apply to everyone, even if you do not agree with them.

Because of all this, always ask to review the regulatory documents before you purchase a condominium, and get help in analyzing how they will affect you. Give a great deal of thought to what you are actually getting, and see if it measures up to what you want.

Key Point

You are not always king or queen of your castle. Do not fool yourself about what you are buying.

Chapter 3

THE ASSESSMENT STREAM—THE FINANCIAL HEALTH OF A HOMEOWNERS' ASSOCIATION

■ What are assessments, and do I have to pay them?

■ When I bought this condominium, no one told me anything about dues or assessments that had to be paid. No one told me they could be increased or that the board could charge special assessments on a whim. Do I really have to pay?

■ What is the association board thinking when it tries to collect delinquent assessments? It feels like they are out to get me!

■ Who makes decisions about regular assessments?

■ What are the limits of regular and special assessment increases?

■ Can the board raise assessments without regard to what the owners want?

■ How many emergency or special assessments may be imposed? Are there limits?

■ Can a homeowners' association decide how I pay my assessments? Can it require that I use automatic bank deductions, a certain bank, or only money orders?

■ Is documentation of need required to issue a special assessment? Is small claims court a viable collection option?

■ How interconnected are my finances if I am an owner in an association?

■ Our homeowners' association board raises the dues every year, without a break! We have so much money in our accounts that we have to approve a resolution every year to carry over the excess, but none of it ever comes back to us as owners. Our dues are so high that we have trouble marketing our homes. The place across the street charges only about 30% of what we pay. What can we do? Can we revolt and stop paying at some point?

■ Our homeowners' association board has not raised the assessments in what seems like forever. I hate to complain about low assessments, but this place is starting to fall apart. Roofs are leaking, siding is failing, and our pool has been closed for years, still being readied for improvements. We would have a hard time selling our units; the only attractive quality about them is the paint job the board had done last year to "brighten up the place"—and the fact that our assessments are only about one-third of what the people across the street pay. Are we headed for disaster? Should we get out?

■ I just became a board member. We have to balance keeping assessments low so that the units remain marketable to the kind of people who can afford to live here while at the same time collecting sufficient money to meet the obligations of the association, which include maintenance of old buildings with lots of problems. What do we take care of first?

■ What are reserves?

■ Our board just announced that we need to pay an extra $100 a month for the next three years to get the level of reserves up—is this common?

■ Why is it important for boards to be assertive about collections?

■ May a board borrow from reserves accounts?

■ Is foreclosure ever justified?

■ What are some of the arguments on the question of whether nonjudicial foreclosure should be allowed for nonpayment of HOA assessments?

■ Why is there so much bad press about homeowners' associations?

■ Where is the concept of foreclosure for the collection of delinquent assessments headed?

■ The management company has a policy to charge $75 for a copy of the association common area pool and gate keys. Is it legal to charge these kinds of extra fees in homeowners' associations?

What are assessments, and do I have to pay them?

Assessments are money collected from the condominium owners by the association—usually on a monthly basis—to take care of costs associated with the upkeep and repair of common-area parts of the association, like keeping the sidewalks shoveled in the winter. In a condominium-ownership situation, there will be *assessment requirements* provided in the Declaration of Restrictions. You will have to pay your fair share, whatever that is, and if you do not, in many states the association has the right to take your property.

When I bought this condominium, no one told me anything about dues or assessments that had to be paid. No one told me they could be increased or that the board could charge special assessments on a whim. Do I really have to pay?

Sometimes people who purchase condominiums really do not know anything about assessments. Sometimes it is just a matter of denial. Some new buyers are not told about assessments when they buy from relatives or friends, or if the sale did not go through a legitimate escrow. In those cases, the buyers do not find out about the assessments until the homeowners' association starts sending notices. Sometimes the past due debt is quite high, and the new owner asserts that it is not his or her debt and believes that the association will not be able to collect the assessments owed.

Failure to pay your assessments is very serious, and

> ### Key Point
> Failure to pay your assessments can lead to very serious consequences, including a lawsuit or even foreclosure on your condominium.

homeowners' associations in many states have the authority equivalent to a lender, meaning they can actually foreclose on your condominium if you do not pay your assessment debt, even without going to court. If an owner in a condominium development does not pay his or her share of assessments, the debt can grow without the owner being aware of it. Homeowners' associations are often entitled to add collection costs to the assessment debt, which can add up quickly if the owner ignores the debt. Some states, such as California, have laws that require associations to meet with owners who are behind in their assessment payments if the owner requests a meeting. Some associations allow payment plans so owners can catch up with their payments. Other associations do not take either action and require the debt to be paid all at once.

What is the association board thinking when it tries to collect delinquent assessments? It feels like they are out to get me!

The general public—lacking full understanding of the reality of association financial requirements and obligations—is not enamored by the idea of assertive or aggressive collections. But your board does have a legal duty to take reasonable steps to collect the delinquencies. After all, failure to do so is money out of your pocket.

Foreclosure is not a favored word, but it may be necessary in a society where people do not live within their means, banks stretch financing beyond many people's capabilities, and the economy goes up and down like a roller coaster ride.

People can usually understand when a lender forecloses on a house or condominium if the owner does not pay the mortgage. If the mortgage is not paid, it hurts the lender. But the general public does not understand the value of having the possibility of foreclosure available to an association. In a homeowners' association, if assessments are not paid by someone, it hurts the fellow members of the association and the complex as a whole, because even if an owner does not pay, the board still is required to maintain the condominium and provide insurance and other amenities.

> ### Key Point
> If any owner does not pay his or her assessment, the board still is required to maintain the condominium and provide insurance and other amenities—the rest of the members may have to pay what is missing from the budget.

The idea that an association should have so much power does not sit well with many people. When the average person hears about a foreclosure in the news, his or her sympathy is probably with the person who is ousted from his or her home. Legislators bristle and continue to whittle away at the rights of homeowners' associations when prompted by the consumer advocacy groups. The newspapers have a heyday criticizing associations that foreclose. It is easy to hate the association, the big guy against the little guy—it is a popular position to take. However, associations have obligations in managing an organization. The association has bills to pay, infrastructure to maintain, insurance to purchase, and the necessity of professional help to ensure compliance with complicated laws, and any association that does not actively collect delinquent assessments can find itself in a bind.

The diligent collection of assessments is a matter of fiduciary responsibility, and the board is the fiduciary. In the long term, a failure to diligently collect assessments can lead to numerous problems. In many condominium associations, each member carries an equal obligation to pay assessments. So it stands to reason that if any member does not pay his or her fair share, the others must pick up the slack, or some of the services have to go. Furthermore, if a board lets an owner get too far behind in assessments without pressuring him or her to pay up, the ability to catch up gets further and further out of reach for that owner. Another thing the board has to make sure of is that it is diligent in getting a lien against property for which there is a delinquent debt. If the board fails to do so, the association could lose its protected standing in a bankruptcy or any other kind of action that puts creditors in line.

The board's interest is in collecting the debt; that is its job. Most boards try to do everything they can to locate owners and get them to be accountable and pay their assessments. But when that fails, the board is left with few choices, especially when the owner

> ### Key Point
>
> One of the biggest myths is that associations are anxious to foreclose on unfortunate owners' property. The truth is that in a huge majority of cases, properties that are in collections from associations do not end up being foreclosed.

does not come forward and propose a way to get the debt cleared. The situation becomes a catch-22 because if an association does not collect assessments from an owner, the other owners have to make up the difference. If the board stays on top of delinquencies and is firm in its policies, all owners are less likely to get too far behind to catch up. They are less likely to face the threat of losing their homes, the association is more likely to be able to pay its expenses, and the homeowners who are paying the assessments are less likely to have to pick up the slack.

> **Key Point**
> When one owner does not pay assessments, it creates an unanticipated and unfair burden on the other owners.

If you really think it through, it makes sense. *Most people who purchase condominiums want their neighbors to pay their assessments and to pay them on time.* Why? Because if their neighbor does not pay, then they will have to pay more than their fair share—someone has to make up the difference. The effect can be felt by everyone if 10% or more of the owners in any given association are chronic late-payers or do not pay their assessments at all. The size of the association or assessment does not matter—a 10% dent in the budget has an effect. The board either has to make a decision to drop some services, cut expenses, or collect more from the other owners. And if the association needs to do some major work and wants to get a loan to allow members to cover a large expense with monthly payments rather than a special assessment, the loan could be very difficult to obtain with a high percentage of delinquencies. The bottom line is that a board has to stay on top of collections to fulfill its duties as fiduciaries for all the association members.

Who makes decisions about regular assessments?

Generally, the board determines what the assessments will be for the coming year and sends out a budget to the members. However, in some states and in some governing documents, the members are allowed to vote whether to approve the budget. If this is the case, and the budget is not approved, it is sent back to the drawing board.

If the association is in a state that does not require member approval and the documents do not require member approval of the budget, the board should not submit the budget for a vote by the members. Why? Each member votes on the budget from an individual perspective, but the board has to look at the budget from the standpoint of what is best for the whole community. And in many cases, the law or the governing documents require that the board adopt the budget and send it to members within a certain time frame before the fiscal year begins. If the board allows the members' voting to interfere with that time frame, it can, in some cases, have a detrimental effect because there can be ramifications if the budget does not go out on time. Some laws prohibit increasing the assessments if the budget does not go out on time and owners are not notified of the next year's assessment by a certain date. That means, if an increase is needed and the board cannot implement it, something has to go.

It also does not make sense to create unnecessary stress during the budgeting time of the year. If the owners vote the budget down, the board or the association could be subject to legal action (maybe even a lawsuit) because the board is charged with the obligation of collecting sufficient funds to meet the needs of the association.

What are the limits of regular and special assessment increases?

There usually are limits on how much a board may increase the regular assessments that are paid for operating costs and contributions to the reserves each year without a vote of the members. If a vote of the members is required, the approval requirement will be stated either in the state law or in the governing documents most likely as either a *majority of the owners* or a *majority of the quorum* of the owners. These are two very different requirements. A majority of the owners is generally more than one half of all the owners of units (counting one vote per unit). A majority of a quorum is different. If a *quorum* of owners (which would have to be comprised of more than half of the unit owners) votes on something, sometimes a majority of those voting can determine the outcome of the election. That would be a majority of a quorum. It is confusing, but it is important to understand that there is a distinct difference between the two approval requirements. In the case that the requirement is a majority of the owners, the deciding vote would require 51% of all members. In the case that the requirement is a majority of the quorum, the deciding vote could conceivably be made by 26% of the members because if at least 51% of the owners vote, the majority of those voting is enough to carry the measure.

There are also usually limits on how much a board may charge for any special assessments without a vote by the members. If a vote by the members is required, it will be stated either in the state law or in the governing documents—again, most likely as either a majority of the owners or a majority of the quorum of the owners, or, in similar requirements, based on ownership interests rather than the number of owners. The percentage of a vote required will probably be

> ## Key Point
> State law and the regulatory documents commonly dictate limits on assessment increases that can be made without the approval of the members. If the state law and the regulatory documents differ from one another, the deciding factor as to which authority takes precedence in one state may not be the same as in a neighboring state.

consistent with the percentage required for the operating costs, the exception being in some cases in which there are different approval percentages for special assessments, which is especially common in the case of widespread damage and destruction. Sometimes these percentages are based on square footage.

Can the board raise assessments without regard to what the owners want?

There is, in most states and in most documents, a right vested in the board of a homeowners' association to impose some form of an emergency assessment on all owners (or in some cases, individual owners) if something happens to the major components or structures that, without being addressed on a rather immediate basis, could pose a safety issue or hazardous condition. The imposition of an emergency assessment usually requires at the very least (1) specific findings; (2) proper notice to owners; and, (3) proper backup documentation in the files.

In most cases, one expects that the right to impose an emergency assessment would be based on the fact that the condition that requires fixing (maintenance, repair, or reconstruction) is not something that was evident during budgeting time. Otherwise, people ask questions as to why the board did not consider the expense at that time. In some states, the imposition of an emergency assessment that would be exempt from the regular and special assessment parameters might also include assessments imposed as a result of a court judgment against the association. Some associations have imposed emergency assessments to pay for unanticipated increases in insurance premiums, to pay a deductible, or to reconstruct as necessary, such as in the event of an earthquake, hurricane, or other serious and damaging event.

The questions to ask are:

• Does the state law allow for the emergency assessment, without member involvement in the decision?

• Do the governing documents allow for the emergency assess-ment, without member involve-ment in the decision?

Key Point

State law and/or the regulatory documents may allow for emergency assessments. Even when the assessments can be imposed, there are generally some documented findings at the sites indicating a previous lack of foresight and the need for repair, which justify the expenditure.

• Was the proper documen-tation collected?

• Were proper notices sent to owners?

• Was the emergency assess-ment justified under the law and circumstances?

The following are a few examples of instances where emergency assessments might be justified (assuming the authority to impose an emergency assessment exists in your state law or documents).

• A deck on one of the units comes crashing down, a resident puts his or her foot through a step on the stairs leading up to the building, or the elevator freezes up and the repair involves a large sum of money and attention immediately. In any of these cases, the board, upon diligent investigation and consultation with the right kind of experts, may find that the problem is isolated or widespread and measures may have to be taken to prevent accidents or the inability to get to and from the units that require a special assessment.

• The earthquake or property insurance policy for coverage of the buildings on the property has just come in at triple the cost of the prior year's premium, the board has thirty days to make a decision about continuing coverage (not enough time for an informed vote by the members), and the regulatory documents for the association require the coverage.

• The court just approved a judgment of $1 million over and above the maximum insurance proceeds available in an action against the association brought because of an accident in the common area, defamation of association vendors, or some other incident, and the judgment is allocated equally among all homeowners.

• The city or county has just come in and decided that some improvement or fix is required that involves major construction in order for the association to continue to receive water, sewer, fire response, or other necessary services provided by the city or county.

The following are a few examples of instances in which emergency assessments probably would *not* be justified (assuming the authority exists in your state law or documents to impose an emergency assessment).

• The board decided to add a spa to the swimming pool, got a bid, and had thirty days to respond. The contract was signed and the board now needs the money—quickly.

- The board knew that the insurance premiums were going to double, triple, or quadruple the next time they came due, and yet it based its estimate in the budget costs for the coming year on the premium just paid, and then waited until the notice came in and declared an emergency.

- The board decides to fix the decks or stairwells and collect an emergency assessment to do it, but decides that while they are at it, they might as well complete the siding and painting project because it will have to be done anyway when the decks and stairwells are reconstructed. The board then increases the emergency special assessment to cover all costs without seeking member approval of the assessment.

How many emergency or special assessments may be imposed? Are there limits?

There are limits on the assessments that can be imposed and on increases in the regular assessments in most, if not all, jurisdictions. Boards do not have unfettered authority to demand and collect money from the members of an association. Limits are usually stated in the state laws and often also in the regulatory documents. Sometimes the two conflict, and then the *hierarchy of integrity* (which set of laws has precedence over the other) must be determined.

Most associations estimate the budget for the coming year and send out notices of assessment increases and special assessments with the pro forma budgets, as the time frames for giving notice commonly coincide with the budget disclosures. However, life being what it is, events can occur later on that throw a real cog into the works, and the board might realize that it did not estimate enough needs in the budget to cover necessary expenses. Hurricane Katrina is an excellent example. It was the largest natural disaster in

U.S. history and the fallout included, with regard to homeowners' association costs, substantial unanticipated increases in fuel, building materials, transportation, and availability of resources, insurance, and construction costs. Some product costs and insurance premium increases were, in many cases, exponential.

There are times when the increases do not coincide with the fiscal year, such as a case when, halfway through the year, the board finds that the budget is going to fall short of the needs of the association. In any case, the intent should be to provide owners with sufficient notice to allow them to prepare for the new assessment amounts, but circumstances do not always leave adequate time to plan and make it "to the ready" before the big increases come forth.

Can a homeowners' association decide how I pay my assessments? Can it require that I use automatic bank deductions, a certain bank, or only money orders?

Basically, the answer to the question as to whether the board of a homeowners' association can generally determine how assessments are to be paid is yes. The board decides where assessments are to be sent for deposit, and it would probably be considered reasonable in most cases that the board require the assessments to be made in some form other than cash, although it is important to check state statutes and the regulatory documents and board policies because there may be parameters stated. Many associations use bank services these days to collect assessments, meaning they require payments to be sent directly to a bank where they are deposited directly into association or holding accounts.

There may be provisions in the state law or regulatory documents or policies that allow owners who are delinquent in payments to get a receipt for payments, or require that the board provide an address for receipt of overnight payments.

Use of the bank deposit services provides associations with advantages, but it is not easy to get a receipt for any individual deposit. The homeowners' association receives a printout of all receipts, but special arrangements commonly have to be made to retrieve individual deposit information. The generic bulk system for collecting the payment makes sense. That is why many associations require that payments be sent into a bank directly. These processes streamline collections and the record keeping of deposits. This can also save the association money over collection by the bookkeeper or manager, and it serves as a check and balance with regard to control over incoming funds.

If a board wants to collect assessments through deductions from personal bank accounts, it would be convenient for both the board and the condo owner, but the owner must first agree to this form of collection. However, requiring a deduction from a bank account could come under fire. Not everyone wants their homeowners' association or management company to have direct access to their bank accounts. Some owners hold their bank account information very "close to the vest," and prefer to send money orders or cashier's checks. In this day and age of identity theft, that is understandable.

> ### Key Point
> The board can justify more latitude in dictating how payments must be made and whether an instrument must be backed by the bank funds if an owner has a poor payment history.

As for requiring payments to be made by money order, boards might require payments in some form other than checks or cash. Neither management companies nor associations generally are prepared to exchange and make change for cash transactions, or keep records of them. There is simply no efficient way to deal with cash in this kind of business. But requiring a money order over some other form of payment, such as a personal check, could be taking things too far. On the other hand, in a case where an owner has been chronically delinquent in his or her assessment payments and the board distrusts the capability of the owner to follow through on keeping his or her account current, it is conceivable that the board might require negotiable payments or automatic deductions so that it does not have to continually deal with the aspects of chronic late payment.

Is documentation of need required to issue a special assessment? Is small claims court a viable collection option?

The best strategy for a board to justify assessments is to document, document, and document some more—the need, purpose, basis for, etc. However, many boards do not know this. If there is no documentation, it may be difficult for a board to defend the need for a special assessment and an owner may be successful in challenging it. This is not an uncommon question or proposed course of action. Small claims court is an option for challenging what you believe is an unfair or unjustified assessment. However, be sure to ask for the documentation, in writing, first. The hearing officer or judge will want to see that you requested the documentation. States have different upper monetary limits for the court actions and different processes that allow laypersons to test their own claims in courts of smaller dollar limits. Common limits are $5,000 or $7,500, and sometimes the upper limit

Key Point
The idea behind utilizing small claims court whenever possible is that it can be a viable vehicle for resolving conflicts without the necessity of hiring an attorney for every legal dispute. The flip side, though, is that the remedies are limited.

can change if a person or plaintiff files more than a certain number of claims in a given year. Most such courts of smaller jurisdiction have programs that allow a *plaintiff* (the person bringing the claim) assistance with forms and processing, including help with the complaint form, subpoena of records, etc., without cost.

The idea is that individuals should not be required to hire attorneys for every legal dispute. If an owner is upset about an assessment charged, he or she can probably file a small claims complaint and have the matter decided by an objective, neutral hearing officer of some kind (whatever the court system offers). One person cannot usually pursue claims for others, meaning if you are an owner who wants to challenge a special assessment charged to you, you could do it (the success factor depending wholly on the case you present and justification for the challenge), but you could not get relief if you want the entire assessment invalidated for others in the association as well.

The purpose of allowing people to make claims in small claims courts is to limit the hearing to the particular individual's (or company's, if the company is the plaintiff) claim. The process does not allow for attorney representation so as to keep the costs down (and fur from flying!). The upper dollar amount is limited so that big dollar claims are not brought into the small claims venue. This does not mean that neither side is entitled to seek legal advice before filing, or to get help from an attorney with preparation for the small claims hearing. But the point is to provide a venue where laypeople can bring their complaints in,

> ### Key Point
>
> Since the *defendant* is the party that is called into court by the *plaintiff*, and thus did not ask to be there, he or she usually has the ability to appeal the decision. If the appeal is successful, the party that sued has to accept the decision as is.

have a knowledgeable legal advisor or judge hear both sides, and receive a decision in the matter. In most cases, the venue brings finality to a legal question about who is right and who is wrong.

Since the defendant is the party that is called into court by the plaintiff, and thus it is not the choice of the defendant to be there, the defendant has more options than the plaintiff. Most, if not all, small claims court jurisdictions allow a defendant who loses in small claims court to request another hearing (to *appeal* the decision) that takes place before a judge, sometimes called a *trial de novo*. In addition, anyone who is served with a small claims court complaint as a defendant can generally (with or without an attorney) have the matter pulled up to a court of higher monetary jurisdiction to be decided. Although it is more common than not, one cannot presume that filing in small claims court and getting a decision will be the end of things—it is an option that is available, not a guarantee that it will end the dispute.

It does seem odd that a board would not tell the owners what the special assessment is for. In some "real life" situations, the board has told owners in various ways, via newsletters, meetings, etc.— but the owners who did not attend the meetings or read the newsletters remained in the dark. Neglecting to make assessment information available to owners is definitely *not* the way to go.

If a board needs to consider a special assessment, it typically has some authority to impose one (within limits—see the previous questions in this chapter) that does not require member approval.

> ### Key Point
>
> Before expending the time and energy to file a small claims court action, it is always good to try and resolve the problem. The hearing officer will normally ask how you tried to resolve it if you are the person that filed the claim.

A rather common limit is less than 5% of the budgeted gross expenses for the association for the fiscal year in which the assessment is imposed. If the assessment for all the units exceeds the stated limit, membership approval is commonly required, in percentages listed in the state statute or the regulatory documents. In order to get that approval, the board would have to explain the need. Otherwise, the owners would not likely approve it.

Before expending the time and energy to file a small claims court action, other steps should be taken.

- A list of questions could be presented in writing to the board.

- A member could ask the board to call and address the need at a special membership meeting (town-hall type or otherwise) or through a communication to owners.

- A member could ask for financial and other records related to the special assessment.

Members of associations commonly have the right to request and review association financial records. Ask for records relating to the special assessment. Owners have rights, and there are often fines or other punishments for withholding financial records. In some states and in some regulatory documents, owners have the right to petition the board and ask for a meeting on any valid association-related subject. Find out what rights exist in your situation before going to court. The hearing officer will probably ask you what you did to try and find out about the justification for the special assessment. If you tried, and no information was given, add a records and meetings request to your request for judgment.

Truth be told, many boards will discuss needs for a special

assessment *ad naseum* at board meetings and in newsletters, and owners still do not pay attention (see the next chapter on apathy for more information). The majority of owners do not come to meetings or read newsletters. It is not ever in the board or members' best interests to minimize information about the need for a special assessment. On the contrary, it is best to *maximize* communications for purposes of *buy in* and *acceptance*. People can usually understand need; what they cannot understand or

> ## **Key Point**
> The best defense in small claims court is a cohesive, believable, organized, justified, and heartfelt presentation of your position. The best offense is the same. In many areas, there are small claims advisors available to help you organize your case—for free. The advisors are not advocates, but they can assist a person in understanding a cohesive way to prepare a case.

readily accept are secrets. However, many board members shy away from being the bearer of bad news to their neighbors. They just want to do their duty—quietly—and go forth.

If an assessment imposed on the members exceeds what can be assessed without a vote of the membership it should be considered illegal and unenforceable. If it qualifies as an emergency assessment it might not necessarily be illegal (again, depending on whether the legal requirements were satisfied). These are things to be sure of before traipsing down to court.

So, it is best to ask the questions beforehand, make the effort to get the information, and document your efforts so you do not end up in small claims court with egg on your face. If you are going to go to court, you may as well go with two causes of action instead of one, i.e., a claim of illegal assessment and a claim of failure to provide records under the statute. There is a possibility of penalty for each violation.

How interconnected are my finances if I am an owner in an association?

In any homeowners' association where the owners share amenities and the responsibility for maintenance and operations costs, and especially in a condominium development, how interconnected everyone's finances are is a fact that some people, after purchase, come to regret. Since condos are often marketed as opportunities for carefree living or as properties where you can pay one fee and get it all, the concept that you will be pooling your money with the rest of the association should be evident. When the time comes to ante up, however, the lines can be drawn in the sand.

Our homeowners' association board raises the dues every year, without a break! We have so much money in our accounts that we have to approve a resolution every year to carry over the excess, but none of it ever comes back to us as owners. Our dues are so high that we have trouble marketing our homes. The place across the street charges only about 30% of what we pay. What can we do? Can we revolt and stop paying at some point?

The following is the counterpart—the question that the owners across the street may be asking.

Our homeowners' association board has not raised the assessments in what seems like forever. I hate to complain about low assessments, but this place is starting to fall apart. Roofs are leaking, siding is failing, and our pool has been closed for years, still being readied for improvements. We would have a hard time selling our units; the only attractive

quality about them is the paint job the board had done last year to "brighten up the place"—and the fact that our assessments are only about one-third of what the people across the street pay. Are we headed for disaster? Should we get out?

First of all, money that is collected by the association for maintenance and operations is called *assessments* and not *dues* for a reason. Assessments, unlike dues, are not payments one makes to belong to a club; assessments are more like a tax, similar to that which a municipal maintenance district would collect, to be used for specific and important purposes. The difficulty for the board is finding the balance between charging the right amount of assessments for the needs of the association and keeping the units within market range for the anticipated consumer. Sometimes, this inquiry dictates the need for a discussion as to whether an increase in the regular assessment or a one-time special assessment is better for the association.

And this is not an easy task—see the question from the board's perspective.

I just became a board member. We have to balance keeping assessments low so that the units remain marketable to the kind of people who can afford to live here while at the same time collecting sufficient money to meet the obligations of the association, which include maintenance of old buildings with lots of problems. What do we take care of first?

The financial obligations and responsibilities of everyone who purchases a condominium become connected, and the decisions are made largely by the elected (or appointed) board.

Owners seldom think about the connectivity between everyone living in a homeowners' association. And it generally does not become a problem until assessments begin to go up every single year, more than 10–20% annually; there is a large special assessment imposed; or, a problem is unveiled that alters the financial picture drastically and the notice comes out to members. It is then that owners start asking the question as to

> ### Key Point
> The reality of owning in a home-owners' association is that decisions are made by someone else; namely, volunteers who are willing to serve on the board. If you are not willing to serve, you do not get to make any decisions. You will get to vote on some things, but not on all issues.

whether they can segregate their funds in protest, which is not a viable option.

What are the issues here? For one thing, the association has expenses an owner in a single-family, non-homeowners' association residence does not, such as the cost of operations and administrative expenses of the association, commercial liability and property insurance requirements for property of the whole group, and often the cost of maintaining common amenities. Associations have to pay commercial rates rather than residential rates for property coverage, so it tends to be more expensive. There are property maintenance and management expenses that owners do not have if they live in a non-homeowners' association subdivision. There are reserves that have to be set aside and owners in non-homeowners' association housing tend not to save with the same diligence (perhaps because there is no statutory or documentary obligation). And sometimes the stupidity or inept ability of boards to make good financial

> ### Key Point
> Board members are volunteers, often untrained and unsophisticated in business terms and communication skills. The majority lack the financial acumen of trained financial planners or business owners.

decisions is costly.

The board members are, after all, volunteers and often lack the financial acumen of trained financial planners or business owners.

When boards act prudently, and in the best interests of the community rather than themselves individually, they have to consider the plight of the "lowest common denominator" as well as the capabilities of the "highest." What does that mean? Owners may well be struggling with little equity and ability to withstand a big expense, such as a new roof when it is needed, so if that is the situation, the board should be making every effort to collect reserves rather than rely on a pay-as-you-go basis. If a board does not plan sufficiently to collect enough money ahead of time to fund the major repairs that are needed periodically for buildings and other infrastructure, it can be disastrous. Why? If the owners cannot withstand a major assessment, the project—which may already be proving difficult and fraught with potential problems—becomes even harder to complete. The money has to be there to pay the contractors.

Buildings are not fine wine—they do not improve with age. They deteriorate. And someone has to pay the price of maintaining them, replacing components as needed, and commonly, upgrading failing systems that have either worn out or proven to be defective.

Boards that do not get help in assessing association needs are another source of problems. And that help does not come cheap.

What are reserves?

Reserves are essentially savings, i.e., money in a bank or any other financial institution intended for use for the repair, maintenance, and replacement of the building, and for other major improvements that the association is responsible for.

Our board just announced that we need to pay an extra $100 a month for the next three years to get the level of reserves up—is this common?

It is not uncommon for an association to be under-reserved. *Reserves* are the money that the developer is supposed to leave with the association, which the association board is supposed to continue to collect and put away for repairs, maintenance, and replacement of all the components that the association is required to maintain. Living in a condominium differs from living in a single-family home that is maintained by the owner in that the owners of the condominiums *have* to save some money. How much you have to save is determined by what the board, usually with the help of professionals, says needs to be put away each year so that things like repairing the roofs and painting can be done when it is time to do it.

You do not have control over the money that you have to save; the association's board of directors does. The amount collected to fund the reserves is in addition to the amount collected to pay operating costs.

Those are the two components that make up the assessments—*reserves allocations* and *operating costs*. In most states, these funds are to be kept in separate bank accounts so there is no "accidental spending" of reserves for operations.

> ### Key Point
>
> A *reserve study* really should be accomplished by a professional or someone capable of determining the condition of the items the association must maintain, the remaining useful "lives" of these items, and how much money should be put away so enough will be available when the major repairs or replacements are needed. A board is expected, and one could argue obligated, to choose the right kind of expert to determine how much money is estimated to be needed to maintain the buildings for the next several years.

Generally, a *reserve study* is accomplished by the board with the help of the right kind of professional to determine what money is estimated to be needed for the next several years, so that when the roof needs to be replaced or the painting and siding work needs to be done, there will be enough money. However, it is important to understand that in many cases there is not enough money when a major repair is needed because of the common problem of dry rot, other hidden conditions, national disasters, or the like that result in higher costs, and so special assessments at that time are also not uncommon.

Why is it important for boards to be assertive about collections?

Failing to be assertive constitutes a breach of fiduciary duty.

May a board borrow from reserves accounts?

In most states, boards of directors may borrow from reserves when there is a need—but if a board does borrow money, it is expected to have a plan to repay it. If operations costs keep coming up that are not in the budget, perhaps the problem is inadequate budgeting. It may be that the regular assessments need to be increased. Continually borrowing from reserves will increase the chances of a reserve shortfall and may lead to deferred maintenance, which often leads to even bigger problems.

> ### Key Point
> It is always better not to borrow from the reserves accounts, but the reality of it is that boards come up short all the time—there are many good (and not so good) reasons. If you are an owner, vigilance is important. Some states require notice to owners before borrowing from the reserves.

The need to continually borrow from reserves to meet shortfalls may indicate a poor collections policy. If the association is continually coming up short in paying the bills, maybe the problem is related to failure to have a good track record in collecting assessments. Here is where owners become divided. The public frowns on heavy-handed collections efforts, but failure to be diligent can have a very detrimental effect on your association's financial health.

Is foreclosure ever justified?

Boards of homeowners' associations have a responsibility to the member owners to be diligent in the collection of the assessments. Sometimes sending letters and meeting with owners who are behind is enough to get them to understand the obligation, but sometimes it takes more. In most states, the homeowners' associations have the right to either sue in court, small claims or otherwise, or to foreclose, using judicial procedures or otherwise. The question often arises as to whether it is fair to foreclose on property in HOAs for nonpayment of collections. It sounds like a horrible remedy in any case, and the very idea of it gets a lot of bad press, but what gets even more press is when foreclosure is used to collect what seems to be a few dollars in delinquencies.

The press all over the country has a heyday every time there is a story about a foreclosure for a small assessment amount. Foreclosure of a home for a very small assessment that is not paid does not happen everyday, and not really very often in the scheme of all delinquencies. Of course,

> **Key Point**
> Foreclosure is considered a heavy-handed type of collection. However, on the flip side, failure to be diligent in collections can have a very detrimental effect on an association's financial health, so a board is generally advised by its professionals to do what it can to collect the outstanding debt. The foreclosure threat is a big hammer.

it is always a sad story, and truth be told, the owner often ends up getting his or her property back, sometimes at a high cost that could have been avoided and sometimes along with a large settlement because of errors in the collections processes.

The *Fair Debt Collection Practices Act* and pieces of legislation in each state have a lot of protections written into them to prevent unfair collection processes and foreclosure without several notices to the owner of the property. Still, it happens. And still, sometimes abundant notices are not enough to get the owner's attention.

Sometimes foreclosure happens because the owners are nowhere to be found. You might then ask if it could happen to a person who is deployed by the Armed Services. States that allow nonjudicial foreclosures require the entity or person authorizing foreclosure to sign a Declaration of Non-Military Service under penalty of perjury at some point before the foreclosure can be consummated, in an attempt to quell such sales. There are special procedures required and limitations imposed if an owner is on active military duty.

To distinguish the forms of foreclosure, a court process requires *personal service* (meaning service upon the person, not by mail or other

Key Point

Nonjudicial foreclosure is accomplished without the courts for banks and mortgage lenders as an option for recovering assets that were not paid for. The reason it has been extended to homeowners' associations in most states is that the assessment stream must be protected because the association cannot pick and choose which units it maintains and which ones it does not.

means) of the complaint to an owner of the property; or, if personal service cannot be achieved with reasonable effort, as a last resort, publishing in the newspaper where the property is located can be used as a method of service. Basically, the owner has to be given the opportunity to appear. If he or she does not, his or her default can be taken and the association can proceed using the court processes.

This notification process does not always require personal service—sometimes it can be given by certified mail, posting on the door of the property, on the entry gate if a key or code is required for entry, etc.

Generally, associations are bound at the very least to the same procedures as the lenders and mortgage holders for collecting debts by liens and foreclosures. Then, often, there are additional requirements for the homeowners' associations that do not pertain to lenders. So there are protections for owners—but do they go far enough?

What are some of the arguments on the question of whether nonjudicial foreclosure should be allowed for nonpayment of HOA assessments?

Many say that foreclosure for nonpayment of a mortgage is fair because there is such a large amount of money involved. But assessments are different. Often, there is a very small amount of money involved given the corresponding size of the foreclosure "hammer." So what is the basis for the dispute?

One very big difference between mortgages and homeowner assessments is that a lender can choose the person they loan to, but an association does not choose its members.

The association has no way of shutting out owners who

> **Key Point**
>
> Lenders are at an advantage over homeowners' associations because they can screen the borrower for financial strengths and ability to pay. This allows the lender a layer of protection in determining the borrower's financial ability to pay the money that is owed, while associations do not have this same benefit.

cannot afford the assessments, nor would it ever be easy to determine who those owners might be. Another difference is that the lender is not required to fix up the property or continue to service a loan that is foreclosing. The association cannot stop maintaining or providing services related to building components on one unit because the owner is not paying assessments. The board can take away pool privileges, but it cannot paint around a unit when it comes time to do the scheduled painting project. It cannot avoid re-roofing one unit when re-roofing the rest.

Another major difference is that if the loan does not get paid, the lender, who chose the debtor in this case, is the only one hurt by it. If a homeowner in a condominium development does not pay the assessment, he or she is essentially hurting all the other owners, because that budget shortfall has an adverse effect.

When it comes to collecting assessments in a serious delinquency, in many cases owners of property in homeowners' associations simply do not believe the association can or should have the power to foreclose, and so they ignore the debt. Few owners do that purposely with their mortgage.

Owners get incensed when they receive notice that the association may foreclose on their property. It is likely that the same happens with the lenders' notices, but most owners know that these notices are coming and understand why.

As for comparing the ratio of debt to collection costs, the costs of collection are a big factor of common disdain. The mortgage payment installments are generally much higher than the assessments. If a bank waits four to six months to start foreclosing, however, the costs charged for the steps in the process, even to the point of foreclosure notices, are usually a small percentage of the actual debt, so they do not seem outrageous.

On the other hand, looking at collection costs in regard to

assessments, if the association starts the foreclosure process four to six months after an owner falls into debt, the collection costs to send the proper letters and record the allowed lien are more often "on par" with or more than the delinquency. That is a hard pill to swallow. However, the work that needs to be done in this kind of foreclosure process is very similar to the work necessary in the case of a mortgage foreclosure, whether the monthly amount of assessments due is $25 or $999. The processes require drafting and preparation of certified letters, and drafting, preparation, and recording of official notices, liens, accountings, etc. So it is not surprising that the costs are similar, whether the amount at stake is big or small.

> **Key Point**
>
> It is troublesome to hear a story of a foreclosure for a $147 assessment debt, whether legal or not. Still, that is much more the exception than the norm. Most foreclosures involve a much more substantial debt. And most collections processes do not go to foreclosure.

How is it possible that one would hear about foreclosure being threatened for a debt that is less than $500? If it happens because the board president did not like the owner, or the attorney or manager was too aggressive, that is not good. It is extremely seldom, however, that any foreclosure lacks justification based on the law of collections. And boards can slack off on collecting debt, but not too much because other owners expect the board to be diligent about collecting outstanding debt. In truth, the stories in the news about foreclosures due to $100 debts—which are very few and far between because it so seldom happens—lack sufficient information for the public to make a reasoned determination as to whether the foreclosure was fair because the debt is understated. By the time any collection action reaches the first steps of foreclosure, costs of collection have been attached. The newspapers do not tell you whether the debtor has ignored the association's requests for payment for months or years. They often say the foreclosure occurred without notice, even when notices were provided and even in cases in which the

> **Key Point**
>
> Some states are stricter than others about nonjudicial foreclosures by HOAs. Removing the option completely or making it more difficult for HOAs to collect the assessment debts has a negative fallout for homeowners' associations.

owner actually thumbed his or her nose at the association.

The threat of foreclosure in homeowners' associations for assessment debt does not commonly result in the sale of the unit. But the threat does usually work, as it commands a certain level of respect that might not otherwise be there. In other words, it is the big hammer of the threat of foreclosure that tends to enhance collection efforts, not the sale of units.

Scheduling a foreclosure sale in a homeowners' association is not taken lightly by anyone. Boards prefer to simply collect the outstanding debt and costs that have accrued in the collection efforts. There are two sides, yet the newspapers seldom point that out. In any case in which one owner does not pay his or her homeowner assessments, the other owners have to pick up the slack. If a board does not diligently pursue the debt, it is doing a disservice to those owners who do pay their assessment fees. It is quite simple.

Why is there so much bad press about homeowners' associations?

You have to take the news for what it is, which in many cases is one-sided, sexy, and sensationalist. It is hard to think of those adjectives in relation to homeowners' associations, but it is true. On any given day, the press can take a bad-facts case and make it a national cause. It is important to read between the lines.

The following discussion illustrates the one-sided bias to every major issue surrounding the collection of assessment debts. It is loosely based on a reported newspaper story about the collection of a debt in a California common-interest development.

The purpose of this portrayal is to show how reporters report and how people think about collections in homeowners' associations, and what they miss. The text preceded by the word "example" relates to the storyline, and the text following the phrases "author comment" and "additional note" represents questions and counterpoints from the author of this book. This example is offered so you can see how important it is to understand both sides of the issue.

Example: When Molly P. got a bill from her homeowners' association demanding back payment for what she contends are unauthorized assessments by an unelected, self-appointed board, she resisted paying.

Author Comment: The owner assumed the assessments were unauthorized, which is a common reaction when an owner does not want to pay, and instead of resolving that question first, she decided to withhold payments—which ultimately lead to collections proceedings.

Additional Note: Withholding assessments is a dangerous game. That is because it is not a legal way of expressing objection to the way the association is run. It is likely to lead to procedures and costs of collection. Many assume that rules such as some states' *law of habitability* (which allows tenants to withhold rent payments when necessary repairs in their residence are not made) apply in an association, but this is not so. It is often a costly position to take.

Example: "It was just a clique that got together and began collecting dues," said Molly, who lives in the unincorporated community north of Riverside. "I didn't recognize them as legitimate."

Author Comment: The question arises: what qualifies this owner to make the determination on whether the assessment was legitimate? Furthermore, what inquiries, if any, were made to resolve the question of the assessment's legitimacy? Assumptions get people into trouble every day.

Additional Note: There are responsible and pragmatic ways to determine if the expenses for which assessments are collected are justified. Association members can:

1. educate themselves and confront the board about its conduct;
2. seek reimbursement of assessments paid in small claims court based on these kinds of theories;
3. hire a lawyer and have him or her write a letter based on evidence;
4. support other candidates for office or run for the board at the next election; and,
5. seek recall of the board.

Example: Seven years later, Molly has filed two small claims court cases and a lawsuit, paid more than $2,000 under protest to stave off threatened foreclosure, and has gone through three attorneys—all over what began as a dispute over a $7 monthly assessment.

Author Comment: One cannot help but wonder what "gone through three attorneys" means. It could mean that the attorneys were the problem, but it also could mean that the owner was difficult or had no case. People can drop their attorneys if they do not like the result—or lack of it—that the attorney is able to achieve; but likewise, attorneys commonly drop clients who do not accept reality or who continue to push or want to fight when they are standing on shaky ground with their allegations or complaints.

Additional Comment: It does look like the small claims avenue was pursued, but the owner apparently lost. If the owner *had* won the two small claims matters, the reporter would have mentioned it because it would have supported the argument that the position the owner took was correct. There were no indications in the story that the owner's refusal to pay assessments was justifiable. All we were told was that she refused to pay, in language that seemed to suggest that the association's actions to foreclose were unfair.

Example: Critics of the power wielded by homeowners' associations say cases like Molly's—those in which minor disputes lead to costly and emotionally exhausting litigation—highlight all that is wrong with common interest developments and the elected boards that oversee them.

Key Point

It is extremely unlikely that withholding assessments will *ever* resolve a dispute or alleviate frustration about the directors or the association. It will only exacerbate the differences.

Author's Comment: It takes two to tango as they say, and this is definitely true in protracted litigation. Litigation is costly by nature. But it is not always driven by the homeowners' association.

Additional Comment: The truth may be, disturbing as it is, that the real problems with common interest developments can be narrowed down to the lack of understanding most people have as to what they are all about; the more pointed focus of owners on rights rather than responsibilities and obligations; and the use of volunteers to collect money, make business decisions, and to try and figure out how to deal with money and people issues without specific training in these areas.

Reporters seldom recognize that homeowners' association boards have serious responsibilities coupled with exposure to liability if they fail in their duties. They are, in fact, charged with many of the responsibilities of local city and county government officials, and yet their job can be even more difficult. They are expected to preserve property values in the development, and are charged with the responsibility to referee disputes between owners and keep the peace. And they are made up of unpaid volunteers. They do not get compensated—they do not get sick days, paid leave, or vacation pay. Board members do not share the same immunities from lawsuits that municipal officials have. Assessments often do not get the respect that taxes carry. The board positions are not generally coveted. What drives people to serve *can* be self-centered and self-serving reasons. However, many owners step up because it is a job that has to be done and others are not standing in line to do it.

Where is the concept of foreclosure for the collection of delinquent assessments headed?

The idea of foreclosing for nonpayment of assessments is definitely not a popular one. The debate for and against rights of foreclosure for delinquent assessments will continue to rage on. Legislators in every state get the calls: "My homeowners' association is threatening to foreclose—they can't do that, can they?" Legislation is passed that toughens the laws on homeowners' association foreclosures, which is not the case for lenders, simply because the lenders' lobbies against such laws tend to be very strong and well-funded. The assessment-paying owners have the most to lose. Every dollar not collected and every dollar spent on collections of assessments from itinerant owners must be covered by sums from the association accounts. The expenses of the association are not diminished by an owner's refusal to pay. The board must still provide all owners with the same amenities and maintenance whether they pay or not. Associations have to start budgeting for uncollectible debts as the power to collect assessments is further undermined by legislation.

On the flip side, who creates this uncomfortable situation? People get roped into believing that owning property is the be all and end all, but it can ruin a person's life, especially if a buyer goes in with blinders on and no disposable assets in reserve. There are many in society more culpable than a board trying to do its job by assertively collecting money to pay the association bills. If blame is to be placed, it is only fair to cast a greater net. A vicious circle is created when a person with limited means is edged into a property purchase. Creative lending and variable interest-rate loans with negative *amortization* or low-payment limitations with accrued interest allow owners who would otherwise not be able to get into the housing market an opportunity to own property. However, while they do help first-time owners and investors get into properties,

---

Key Point

The responsibility to pay home-owner assessments should be taken very seriously. Do *not* assume that withholding payments because you are upset about what the board is doing or not doing (with regard to maintenance or anything else) is the best choice.

when the housing market takes a downturn or correction, the economy begins to slip backward, Mother Nature rages, or the low variable interest-only loan comes to an end, the property owners that were squeaked in are often forced back out—through lender foreclosure more often than homeowners' association foreclosure. Many owners find themselves overextended in times of economic downturn, and when the foreclosures of lenders increase, the association board's task of collecting assessments becomes harder and harder. Budgets are stressed and services often reduced, or special assessments are imposed just to keep up and meet expenses. It is not a pretty picture, and unfortunately, in the end, the owner—whether it is the owner who is forced out or the owner who has to pick up the slack and pay more—often blames the board for his or her plight.

The management company has a policy to charge $75 for a copy of the association common area pool and gate keys. Is it legal to charge these kinds of extra fees in homeowners' associations?

Assessments are not the only thing that homeowners' association members complain about. Questions sometimes arise about the reasonableness of fees charged by associations. Usually costs for items provided by the association are closely tied to actual costs of the association, which sounds like a hefty fee. However, in the case of keys, besides getting a new key made, there are administrative costs like passing out and retrieving keys, paperwork related to who has them, extra record keeping when keys are lost, and other such issues. The costs could vary depending on whether real keys or key cards are used. Possibly, there are records involving an owner and the tenant involved that would need to be updated. The association might have a history of too many people losing keys, or too many past residents retaining the keys to use the facilities, and it may have to change the locks or systems periodically. Perhaps the board wants to send the message that hanging on to the keys is something to be taken seriously, and replacement carries a hefty price tag.

Sometimes the locks have to be replaced and everyone in the development has to have a new key when a key or key card is compromised, which can also get expensive. A $75 cost to replace keys tends to eradicate the assumption that losing the key is no big deal.

Living in a homeowners' association does trigger some unexpected expenses. Anyone moving in who does not recognize this will most likely get some unpleasant surprises.

Chapter 4

THE PROBLEM OF APATHY

- What is the number one problem in a homeowners' association?
- What is the result of a high level of apathy?
- What is apathetic owner reactionitis?
- I have served on the board in my community for more than ten years, and owners have rarely ever come to meetings. What can we do to get people interested?
- Interest in our association is so pathetic. I have thought about running for the board, but if I do, what can be done to get people excited?
- We recently held an annual meeting; there were no candidates or nominees, and there are now only two board members out of five positions willing to serve. (And there were only six people who showed up for the meeting out of 116 units.) What do we do?
- If we could pay board members, we might get more applicants—can we do that?
- Who reigns when neither the board nor the members come to meetings?

What is the number one problem in a homeowners' association?

The number one problem in homeowners' associations is a lack of participation.

Why is it that homeowners' associations are so widely affected by apathy? It is because of the opening sales pitch. The first thing people hear when they are looking to buy a piece of property in a condominium development is, "Enjoy worry-free living … all of your problems are taken care of … you don't have to worry about a thing … someone else maintains the property for you… ." Naturally, this is what people like to hear, and this is what sticks in their minds, rather than the information in the pile of documents they receive.

It is very easy to become distanced in a common interest development. People do not tend to work outside in their yards, talk across fences, get to know their neighbors, or develop a *community spirit*. People come to rely on the image of condominium living given by the opening sales pitch, in which they can move in worry free, and not take any responsibility in the maintenance or issues that may have a bearing on their property values. Of course, this is not the case for everyone in every association, but it is usually the case in associations where apathy runs high.

It is a busy world, where people can feel too busy to get involved. People buy into homeowners' associations to escape yard work, concerns about maintenance, landscaping, re-roofing, estimating how much money is needed for improvements and upkeep on the structures, etc. No one wants to have to call the gutter person, the plumbers, the painters, the roofers, the pool person, or any other type of repairperson when there is a problem. People want to call the manager, get everything taken care of, move the problem from their plate to someone else's—i.e., get it off their list of things to do. Owners do not want to be bothered with decisions about planting trees, mowing lawns, choosing vendors, attending meetings, voting, serving on the board, confronting their neighbors with complaints about conduct, and so on.

What is the result of a high level of apathy?

When people leave the work and responsibility to someone else and go on about their lives without paying attention to what is happening, there are several potentially problematic results:

> **Key Point**
>
> Believe it or not, *apathy*, which sometimes occurs through complacency, is one of the biggest problems most home-owners' associations face. People who buy property in the development commonly drop off the association's radar once they get settled in, and they rely on the association board to take care of everything for them.

- a large number of residents (owners and renters) who are uninformed about responsibilities;
- a lack of awareness of the community's financial and political health;
- a lack of homeowners who are qualified to serve on the board;
- a lack of interest and pride in the community; and,
- a lack of interest in serving the community.

And in the more serious cases there could be:

- a strain on the people that *are* willing to serve;
- a strain on the budget; and,
- a decrease in property values.

Even if you do not care about the first five issues, you should care about the last three. Keep in mind, however, that homeowners'

associations that are unable to inform and educate their homeowners due to a lack of interest are also generally unable to get a
quorum of homeowners to show up for the annual meeting, either
in person or by proxy; serve on committees; run for the board; or,
pay for professional help that might be needed when the board is
weak, disinterested, inexperienced in business matters, or unedu-
cated. The absence of this participation in a homeowners' community leads to strain for all owners, whether directly (e.g., the same
owners continuously hold the same positions on the board because
no other owners volunteer for the job), or indirectly (e.g., a decision
made by the board leads to a decrease in property values because it
could not obtain enough money from the owners to hire a professional to advise the inexperienced members in making the decision).

The ultimate and worst possible result of apathy—short of no
leadership at all—is that an association may end up in *receivership*,
with someone at the helm who is simply collecting the money and
paying the bills, while neglecting to promote the community, find
the most efficient and effective way to do things, or focus on
enhancing and preserving property values in the development.

What is apathetic owner reactionitis?

Apathetic owner reactionitis is an unfortunate problem that board
members face. Residents commonly go into hibernation—until the
board reaches out to them with a serious plea for a response to an
important issue. That is when the unpleasant reactionitis comes
into play.

Updating or restating the regulatory documents, for example, is
something big. Boards often try to bring the regulatory documents
that can be amended into sync with current laws and make them
useful—only to be met with criticism about processes, time, money,
and hassle in being asked to read proposed documents. Some boards

keep this work close to the vest, believing that the owners are not really interested, anyway. Others work to involve the homeowners, and find it is like pulling teeth to get feedback—that is, until the voting package is sent out.

It is after the voting package is sent out that the vocal minority surfaces. Picture all the critics who believe the saying that the squeaky wheel gets the grease, and you can see how the cacophony could become unbearable. Striving for readable, understandable, and more user-friendly documents can draw unbridled and unjustified criticism for a board that has worked its rear end off at an extremely tedious and important task.

A large special assessment is also an issue that is considered big. Justified or not, it can trigger shouting, fist-waving, ugly notes stuck on doors, tire slashing, and terrible ill-will. Once again, there is the risk of unbridled and unjustified criticism.

It is true that no one except a board member who has served the association for any amount of time can understand the frustration that occurs when members ignore the processes and then criticize the work. The board can work on a project for months, keep the owners informed regularly through newsletters, websites, postings, and communications, and discuss matters at open board meetings, which tend to be lacking in owner attendance, only to find that the members really do care about the big issues—although oftentimes their care manifests itself in the form of complaints.

I have served on the board in my community for more than ten years, and owners have rarely ever come to meetings. What can we do to get people interested?

This is a very common scenario. You may have to dig under the rocks for volunteers, but even going out and recruiting that intensely might not be productive. Having to beg for board members does not guarantee the cream of the crop will turn up.

Most board members are the average Joes in the development. Sometimes board members are representatives of the developer's company—this is most common during the period when the project is being built or expanded, and the developer has a strong interest in keeping control over the budget, maintenance, aesthetics, and information given to new buyers. Obviously, it is in the developer's interest to keep the place nice looking and to keep the assessments as low as possible, at least until all units are sold. There is rarely a shortage of people willing to serve during the period when the development is new. Once the developer is gone, however, the work is turned over to volunteers who do not want a second, non-paying job.

It is work to serve on the board. Finding and grooming capable volunteers for board service is a difficult task (see more in the next chapter). Fighting overall member apathy is equally challenging.

> ### Key Point
> The board vacancies are usually easy to fill, until the developer is out of the picture. This is because the developer has an obvious vested interest in the community. He or she wants to continue to sell units so costs are not spared. However, once the units are sold and the developer leaves, the board pool often dwindles quickly. Like the developer, owners have a vested interest, but do not realize what it takes to keep a smoothly running operation humming along.

Interest in our association is so pathetic. I have thought about running for the board, but if I do, what can be done to get people excited?

There are some ways to try and engage membership. Sometimes you have to be creative.

• **Newsletters or surveys.** Newsletters and periodic surveys can be good ways to provide information and engage owners; they can also be used to elicit feedback from the owners. For example, a newsletter can be used to ask for volunteers to assist on various committees, to announce community clean-up days, to announce social functions or parties, to commend good neighbors, to award prizes or give recognition for service, or to highlight action items in meetings. In this day and age, with so many people having computers and so many simplified publishing programs, most communities could find someone that would be able to produce a newsletter or survey for circulation. Absolutely, however, no *one person* should be authorized to send out or submit the newsletter to the community without editing or careful consideration of what is written by someone capable of spotting trouble. There are legal ramifications to certain actions and statements.

• **Meet-and-greet "welcome wagon" and social activities.** The entire grooming process could be commenced at the very early stage of welcoming new members to the community. A welcoming committee or member could take coupons and other small gift items to new association members and visit with them, ask about their backgrounds and interests, and gather considerable insight as to whether these new owners are interested in becoming part of the community, or are simply looking for something different. At the same time, the person serving in this capacity of welcoming new members could discuss the pool, parking, and pet rules—in a nice way, of course. The worst use of such a welcome wagon is to descend on the new owner, spout out the association rules, and leave.

- **Social activities.** Associations that have social activities during the year tend to have a better community spirit. Some associations have an annual party of some kind, like a Halloween or Christmas party, or an annual barbecue. Some associations combine a social activity with the annual meeting, to bring more people out. Some associations have social hour before the board meetings, but caution is in order. If the association serves any liquor at these functions, it may be asking for trouble. If liquor is served at social functions, make it very light. If you are creating a party situation, it would be wise to check with your insurance carrier to make sure that you have coverage for incidents related to alcohol that is served on community property. Even if you serve a glass or two of wine before an annual or board meeting to those attendees, you are risking an incident, loose talk, and a lack of formality, and any of these can hurt the association. Drinking at meetings also tends to lead to abusive interactions from someone who cannot handle alcohol. If alcohol is served, do so in great moderation.

- **Periodic reporting to the membership.** Even if your association does not have a newsletter or plan social functions, it can keep the community well-informed through the distribution of communications. Each year, associations are required to send out financial and other information, so use this opportunity to include something positive as well.

The board or social committee has to essentially *capture* the community to avoid widespread apathy. It has to continuously work to keep the community interested in what is happening.

It is important when the association needs to put a ballot out to the community that the solicitation materials not only satisfy legal requirements, but that they also thoroughly explain the problem or need for response in layperson's terms. Associations that have lawyers write the solicitation letters without any feedback as to whether even the board can understand what is being said are doing a disservice to the community. Certainly, there are times when attorney input is needed, but in many cases simply having someone from the board jot down his or her thoughts and what is important to him or her—and the more input from the board members, the better—helps get the juices flowing, which leads to ideas and tends to lend a realistic and general flavor that should be carried on into the solicitation materials that go to the homeowners.

After all, the board members do come directly from the community, and if they are pleased with the communication that is directed to the homeowners, chances are the homeowners will be more likely to appreciate and understand it. If the attorney prepares the communication and the board members see it as a bunch of legal jargon, then the homeowners will do the same—if people cannot understand something, they will not read it and they are not likely to respond to it.

> ## Key Point
> If the attorney is asked to send an attorney communication and it is full of legal jargon, it is useless. If people cannot understand something, they will not read it and are not likely to respond to it. And worse yet, many people are put off by attorney communications, so keep these to the barest minimum—zero to none is advisable, unless there is something needed like a lawsuit disclosure.

We recently held an annual meeting; there were no candidates or nominees, and there are now only two board members out of five positions willing to serve. (And there were only six people who showed up for

the meeting out of 116 units.) What do we do?

Can you believe this could happen? Well, it does every day! Perhaps it is a lack of interest, fear of exposure to liability for making decisions, apprehension that taking on a position will cause too much pressure or require a large amount of work, etc. If a board cannot get a quorum at an annual meeting or cannot get enough candidates to fill open positions, it cannot hold a legally valid election. However, many go forward based on practical necessity—a board must take matters to the appropriate level and consider other means of naming directors. If it cannot get a sufficient response to a voting measure that is put to the homeowners—for things like special assessments, amendment of governing documents, etc.—it cannot follow through with important business decisions and properly administer to the community.

If we could pay board members, we might get more applicants—can we do that?

The condominium model is set up to provide for a nonprofit, mutual benefit type of organization run by volunteers. Most original bylaws therefore provide that board members, while entitled to reimbursement for expenses that are incurred in providing service, shall not receive compensation. Why is this? There are many reasons, the main one most likely being that the intention was that the community would govern itself, without the motivation of compensation for service. Volunteers are given protection through statutes in many states simply because they are serving without compensation. Often, developers and investors (people owning more than one or two properties in the same development) are excluded from the protections, being carved out of the definition of volunteer, even if they are not being paid for board service. Some associations have adopted stipends or partial or full assessment reductions for board members. Many do this without regard for the legal consequences, because they do it without consulting an attorney to determine the ramifications. Since important liability protections are commonly forfeited upon receipt of payment or an assessment reduction of any kind, the question becomes whether the compensation really sufficiently makes up for that loss of protection. Furthermore, the payments or reductions in assessments are probably illegal, and subject to challenge and ultimate payback, if they are made without regard to conflicting limitations in the governing documents. Most boards that enact these kinds of benefits for board members are clueless about the trade-off that occurs.

Here are some other ideas that might help beat apathy in an election setting.

- Schedule an association social a month or two before the annual meeting, perhaps a barbecue or a pot luck, and put on the party notice that there will be an open discussion, "On the Future of the Association—Are We Going Uphill or Sliding Down?" This should muster some interest.

- Send out a survey reminding all owners that it is their responsibility to help with service on the association board or in some other capacity, such as by serving on a committee. Ask members about interests and availability, and if they are prepared to pay for more services if there are not enough volunteers to serve in leadership roles.

For the purpose of establishing a legal quorum in order to try to have a legal election:

- Include a proxy with billing statements and encourage owners to return the proxy so it will be at the meetings in the event they cannot be present, and someone else can vote in their place.

- Give as a choice on the proxy a box to check for quorum purposes only.

- Make telephone calls and go door-to-door when a ballot measure is out before the members or an annual meeting is coming up, to get the owners' attention.

Associations are headed for trouble if owners do not step up to the plate and participate, and, more importantly, serve on the board. Sometimes it is difficult to get members to serve because too much time is required. Sometimes it is because owners do not want to get between their neighbors and collections, rules enforcement, etc. Sometimes it is because people do not feel they have the expertise. This is where choosing management might come into play. A board member's duties can be minimized with a good, resourceful management company. If the association is small and does not feel it can afford full-service management, there are in many areas of the country consultation and specific types of management services available. For example, some associations have delegated only the financial management to a professional. Others use management consultant services for violation letters, hearings, etc., related to the enforcement of the documents. Some associations have delegated architectural review to outside consultants. This might be one of those situations

Key Point

A court-appointed receiver, even if diligent and perceptive, is not optimal for an association even if it is down to minimal participation by members. However, if there are not enough members stepping up to serve on the board or members are not willing to pay for management, an association may end up with a receiver.

when it is time to tell the members of the association to either ante up the money for trained management services or for a disinterested court receiver. A *receiver* is a person appointed to carry out business as needed when a viable entity has no one at the helm making the decisions. Is receivership a good alternative to a board? No, it is not. Receivers are costly and do not have the same perspective as the owners who form the association. They pay bills; collect money, sometimes with unfettered power to assess, regardless of documentary limits; and, some have *no* association management experience.

Leaving a ship without a captain, or worse yet, no one at the helm, is a legally actionable error attributable at least to the last man serving, and more likely to the last board serving. However, the loss could accrue to the entire association if the board members left because of member apathy and a general unwillingness to serve, if the board members are protected through indemnification language in the governing documents, or if the directors and officers have insurance coverage. So consider finding another solution if you are one of the remaining board members in your association and are thinking about jumping ship.

In most jurisdictions, a homeowners' association would be a corporation, and there are corporate laws in many states that provide even one remaining board member the power and authority to appoint board members. In the scenario described earlier in this chapter, two out of five board members are not enough to make any decisions for the association, but if they can find a third willing volunteer to appoint, they could be off and running toward a brighter future for the association.

If no owners are willing to serve, and these remaining board members resign and leave

> ## Key Point
> Apathy can lead to disaster. If it is a problem in your association, get help.

no one in charge, it could backfire on them, since there are many bad things that can happen. Eventually, someone will try to sell his or her condominium and there will be no one to fulfill the association's duty to provide seller/buyer-requested escrow documents. People start asking questions, and the real estate agents and the seller come to the conclusion there is no active association. This means that lenders will no longer finance the units because no one collects the assessments, pays the association bills, or arranges maintenance as needed. No one keeps up the state corporate filings, so the association status falls to inactive and the association loses its ability to contract for services.

How can apathy lead to disaster? There are many other problems likely to occur besides a lack of volunteers. No one collects assessments? No one pays the bills? In a condominium, the water or electricity may be turned off. The landscaping will fail if the water is off, the gardeners will quit for failure to get paid, and the pool will become a hazard if the chemicals are not balanced or the levels are not kept up. The buildings or common areas will eventually fall into disrepair. Insurance policies protecting the association, the association members, and the board members will lapse. There will be no insurance in the case of a fire or other casualty, and there will be no insurance to pay for the defense against claims against board members and the association when they get sued for breach of fiduciary duty.

Most governing documents will protect the board members through *indemnification* clauses, but if there is no insurance or money coming in, the board members who left the association in this condition may end up paying the bulk of damages or losses.

People may start constructing otherwise prohibited improvements, stop following parking rules or restrictions, and stop honoring pool rules as a result of apathy. Some things that happen may be irreversible.

There is a host of potential problems, but the worst brunt of things may fall on the last remaining board members for abandoning ship. The choices left to board members who are burned out or owners who determine there is no longer a board include the right to have a receiver appointed, and this may be the direction a desperate board or some of the members need to take.

Sometimes this seemingly hopeless scenario can be alleviated with a letter to the owners warning of the dire consequences of not having anyone willing to step up and serve. The letter can explain that going into receivership is no picnic, and not the best choice for the association. The members will have to pay the cost of a receiver, and, before falling into this situation, should be given the option of paying for association management instead. Good management can relieve board members of the heaviest portion of the burden of volunteer service, which may in turn encourage more service.

As a last resort, before discussing receivership, call every home-owner, or go door-to-door if necessary, to find willing board members who want to avoid the consequences of receivership.

Who reigns when neither the board nor the members come to meetings?

If there is a manager, he or she often takes the lead but is then some-times later criticized for making decisions.

Here are some myths and realities about meetings.

Myth: The fact that everyone stays away from meetings and ignores communications, surveys, and ballots simply means they are all happy with the way the association is being managed.

Reality: In most cases, people have been sold a carefree lifestyle and generally people are too busy to care about what is happening in their association. They do not want to be bothered with details. This can create a false perception that everyone is satisfied and unquestioning.

Myth: Owners who ask a lot of questions or complain a lot are dissident or disgruntled homeowners.

Reality: Everyone has a right to ask questions. Challenging decisions made by the board, or a lack thereof, never endears a member to the board. Some owners who ask questions or challenge the board can be very valuable when enlisted into association service. Few things are worse than a "yes man".

Myth: If there is no quorum, everyone must be sent home.

Reality: When people take the time to come to a meeting, even if there is no quorum to vote on anything, the board can give reports or take the opportunity to poll the attendees and find out what they think on any given topic. Interests can be explored and the value and importance of service (like serving on the board or a committee) can be discussed. This is the benefit of a town hall meeting: allow give and take, identify problems and look for solutions, brainstorm, create goodwill, talk about what happened over the past year, ask for suggestions on getting neighbors to come out, or plan a social event. Most governing documents allow for the board to adjourn a meeting when there is no quorum, and schedule a follow-up meeting.

The proper way to adjourn a meeting is with a motion to the owners present, but the board often just does it. The follow-up meeting should be held within the timelines stated in the regulatory documents, which generally specify the timeline as "not less than five nor more than thirty days without requiring a notice other than announcement at the meeting." Some documents allow for reconvening later the same evening, and some have a lower proxy requirement, allowing the board to achieve a quorum with little door-to-door footwork or filler time while attendees try to round up their neighbors.

If there is no quorum of board members (i.e., for a board meeting) or of members (i.e., for a membership meeting), no actual business can be conducted. It does not preclude using the time for social purposes, but without the quorum, business normally cannot be done. There are exceptions, however, so if you are in an association that is unfortunate enough to be unable to get enough members to vote at elections, you would do well to get some professional advice about how to deal with it.

Chapter 5

THE BOARD— ELECTIONS AND SERVING AS A BOARD MEMBER

- ■ Who are typical board members?
- ■ What is expected of a board member?
- ■ How do I run if I want to serve the board? What do I do?
- ■ What do I need to know about qualifications? What qualifications must I have? Does anyone enforce them?
- ■ What does *good standing* mean, and why would it be required to be on a board?
- ■ What are some of the frustrations of serving on the board?
- ■ Why do people serve on the board if it is such a thankless job?
- ■ What happens when board members face complicated laws?
- ■ What is the worst thing that can happen if a board member strays from the law?
- ■ What if a board member resigns and then takes it back? Is he or she still a board member, or not?
- ■ What happens if all board members want to resign?
- ■ I am a homeowner in a twenty-unit association. Our board is unresponsive to questions, requests, etc. I feel helpless—I cannot find out about anything that is going on. What recourse do I have?
- ■ How does one approach the board with a concern and not anger the directors?
- ■ My board is out of control—is it time for action? What can I do?

Who are typical board members?

Sometimes it seems like board members come from another planet. But most are owners of property in the development. Sometimes board members are representatives of the developer's company—this is most common during the period when the project is being built, and the developer has a strong interest in keeping control over the budget, the maintenance, aesthetics, and what new buyers are told. Obviously, it is in the developer's interest to keep the place looking nice and the assessments as low as possible, at least until all the units are sold. So there is rarely a shortage of people willing to serve during the period when everything is new.

What is expected of a board member?

The board of a homeowners' association generally meets once a month or once a quarter. The meetings take place on-site if there is a place, sometimes in a clubhouse, sometimes in a pizza house, and sometimes in one of the board member's homes. The meetings are usually open to all members of the homeowners' association, with rare exceptions.

How do I run if I want to serve the board? What do I do?

Serving on the board is a commitment. The way to run for the board is to find out when the elections will be and submit your name, take advantage of the option to petition the board if the documents allow for it, or do whatever is needed to get your name to the board on time to have it on the ballot.

What do I need to know about qualifications? What qualifications must I have? Does anyone enforce them?

Here are some possible qualifications your association may require for board membership (again, be sure to consult the regulatory documents to see what applies in your community).

- A director must be a *member* (owner) of the association.

- A director must be in *good standing*. (That usually means current in their assessment accounts and in compliance with the regulatory documents and rules of the association.)

- A director must take courses specifically designed for directors of community associations.

- Each director must walk the complex once each calendar quarter and provide to the membership and board a written report of the condition of the complex.

Of course, if qualifications are adopted and enforced, the flip side is that the pool of possible volunteers for the board will shrink. If your association has apathy problems, requiring that board members take extra time to go to classes might deter some worthy candidates. On the other hand, it makes sense that members who are willing to get some valuable education may make better board members. Thought must be given to whether the qualifications for the board are realistic, meaning they can reasonably be achieved, and whether they are fair. For example, with required educational courses, there are questions that arise, such as, is it readily available? Who will pay for it? Is it fair to require extra work to qualify as a board member? After all, board members *are* volunteers.

What does *good standing* mean, and why would it be required to be on a board?

Good standing is usually defined as being on time with payments of assessments, and not in violation of any governing document provisions. Sometimes it is written more broadly and sometimes more

> ### Key Point
> A *good standing* requirement for board service or voting rights may be defined in the governing documents differently, but it usually means being current in regard to payments of assessments, and not in violation of any governing document provisions.

narrowly. The reason a status of good standing is a qualification for board service is that it should assure that the board members are not bad examples in the community. If a director has not been paying assessments, or is in violation of the rules, it becomes difficult to enforce those requirements upon the other members of the association.

In addition, to be a good candidate for a board position, an owner should attend board meetings, read communications, stay abreast of what is happening in the association, bring ideas to the board if he or she has them, volunteer to serve on committees, and be a part of the community. These are the things that prepare an association member to run for the board.

What are some of the frustrations of serving on the board?

- **Time.** Board service can take a few hours a month or many hours a month. The more organized a board is, the less time serving on the board will probably take. Some boards have preparation and meetings down to a science, even implementing a timed agenda so that meetings are limited to a couple hours. If board members do their homework, read their *board packets* before meetings, and pay attention, things work more smoothly. A board packet is something managers usually prepare for boards, which generally consists of material related to the business that is to be discussed. If there is no professional manager, usually one board member will do the work necessary to collect the materials for the packet. Sometimes each board member brings to the meeting whatever documents or backup materials they need supporting whatever they were supposed to be doing. Copies of the materials brought to the meeting should be kept as association records.

- **People.** Serving on the board can be a thankless job. If giving service as a volunteer does not do it for you, then maybe it is sufficient incentive to want to have a say in what happens in regard to your property. Of course, you will have a say in what happens to the other properties in the development as well. You cannot carve out decisions around your own property. Dealing with the other members can be great, or it can be a royal pain. Other members of the association are not always complimentary. In fact, a board member will probably hear more complaints than kudos during the term of service. Apathy is another people problem—board

> **Key Point**
>
> Most board members will hear more complaints than kudos during their term of service.

members complain that they cannot get owners interested in what is happening in the development. And, of course, there are also the people who complain about neighbors, noise, dogs, harassment, the landscaping, the rules, the budget, the financials, the assessments, and so on.

Why do people serve on the board if it is such a thankless job?

There are many reasons a person might serve on a homeowners' association board. Sometimes it involves a sense of duty; sometimes it is because everyone else took a step back and that left a person out in front of the line to volunteer. Sometimes an owner wants to take up a cause, gets excited about an issue, does not like the way the current board is doing things, believes he or she would make a good leader, or gets roped in when attending a board meeting when no one else is in the audience.

> **Key Point**
>
> Studying the art of communicating with people, active listening, and how to deal with difficult people will help with the people side of serving on the board, which is critical in interacting successfully with other directors and with the membership at large.

Some people are natural-born leaders and feel it is their place, and some just end up on their boards because a friend enlisted them because he or she needed an ally on the board. There can be many different reasons, and you can find yourself serving on a board with quite a diverse group of people, with a large variety of skills, interests, and motivations.

A few classes in dealing with people and active listening should help immensely. Classes that offer training in mediation skills can help a lot in this regard. A board that consists of people willing to review the board packets, listen to each other, express views and then move on, consider things rationally, and act professionally is a good board. A board that consists of strong-willed, argumentative people cannot accomplish much. It helps immensely if the board consists of directors who are good at managing and

> **Key Point**
>
> Attending board meetings is a good way to see what goes on at meetings, how they are structured, and what does or does not get accomplished. This can help you determine whether you want to help by providing service or whether you think you fit the bill for the board.

supervising other people as well as managing resources.

Make sure you want to serve on the board before you put your name into the nomination pool or agree when asked by the board to accept an appointment for a position that has opened up because of a resignation or some other reason.

Here are a couple very possible scenarios that would be difficult for a board to handle unless it had members with training in communication, interaction, or other kinds of proper people skills, especially if the association is unmanaged:

- A newly elected board member comes to his or her first board meeting and finds that the board members are catty and do a lot of name calling, or that a couple of association members sit in the front row and harass the board for the better part of the meeting.

- A member of the association who has proven to be very difficult, abusive, threatening, or controlling comes in with a handful of proxies to the annual election and is elected to the board. The other board members are certain they cannot work with him or her.

Resignations abound in these situations. Volunteer board members often react to what is in front of them, without thinking about the consequences.

Unless your board offers training, stepping into a slot can be an uncomfortable eye opener. You can always resign if you cannot handle it, but that is not an enviable option for you or for the other board members. And if things get dicey and you are one of two remaining board members and there are five total slots, running the board can be really challenging. For example, getting a quorum for board actions is not possible without appointing another board member. Sometimes board members cannot even figure out what they want or what kind of action to take.

What happens when board members face complicated laws?

Many board members in homeowners' associations that do not have professional management (and some that do) are fed up, tired, and want to quit. The laws are overwhelming—seriously overwhelming. Board members picture the "feds," the state, the other board members, and the association members all lying in wait for them to do something wrong. They can become fed up with having the burden placed upon them to make decisions in the best interest of the association, and then with the arguments that follow in the decision-making process and as a result of the decision that is made (e.g., "The costs are too high to get a reserve study done"; or, "The members will not like it if we spend the money to purchase a more expensive kind of insurance").

What is the worst that can happen if a board member strays from the law?

A board that does not follow the law subjects the entire association to legal claims for damages of any kind (e.g., monetary losses, loss in the value of homes, personal injury, etc.), and monetary fines in some cases, as some state laws provide that homeowners' associations or boards can be fined for records inspections rights violations, meetings violations, elections

Key Point
A board that does not follow the law exposes the association to multi-faceted legal claims for damages.

violations, and similar violations.

A board that *knowingly* does not follow the law can lose the protections provided by insurance for board members' actions. *Negligence* (e.g., accidental mistakes, good faith, etc.) is typically one of the components of the liability coverage for board members, and knowingly violating the law is neither an accident or indicative of good faith.

A board that purposely ignores the law can lose the protections provided by statutes commonly known as *safe harbor* laws that offer protection or a layer of legal insulation for members who act in good faith.

Homeowners' associations incorporated as *non-profit mutual benefit corporations* are often under the jurisdiction of the attorney general's office, which means that failure to follow the law can bring down the attorney general's hammer. This is not as likely as receiving a reprimand from the non-profit membership, because the attorney general's office often responds that it does not have the resources to pursue homeowners' association member complaints—but still, this possibility should not be ignored.

When a board member or manager says something like, "Well, everyone else is ignoring the law, so why can't we?" think about it—if you choose to drive 95 mph down the freeway in a 55 mph zone because everyone else is doing it and you get caught, what do you think the police officer is going to say? Probably something along the lines of, "I

> ### Key Point
>
> Not knowing homeowners' association law is understandable to a degree, because it can be hard to find the resources to learn and it is more complicated than the speed limit. Some might get off with a slap on the hand for a minor violation, but ignoring the law when you are a fiduciary is much more serious.

caught *you* and I am going to throw the book at *you*". On the other hand, if you are going 55 mph in a zone you were not aware was really a 45 mph zone and no one is around, the police officer might just let you off with a warning, especially if you say, "Sorry officer, I did not know this was a 45 mph zone". What the officer is probably trying to determine is whether you really did know the speed limit or made an innocent mistake, or maybe even whether you were going to be honest. Just because everyone else is doing it does not make it right.

Not knowing or ignoring the law can have serious ramifications for an association and each board member who is guilty of it. It can have a fallout that reaches other board members if the majority of the board chooses to ignore the law, and, in the worst cases, it can lead to individual liability on the part of the board members, possibly extreme and unanticipated special assessments for the members, and maybe even *punitive damages*.

Board members need to make an effort to learn what to do, when to get professional help for the association, and, although the laws are complicated, they need to resist the temptation to simply hope they will not get caught. Board members are *fiduciaries*, meaning they hold a position of trust that comes from being responsible and having authority over association funds and fiscal responsibilities. Turning your back on the law as a board member is much more serious than ignoring a speed limit sign.

What if a board member resigns and then takes it back? Is he or she still a board member, or not?

Sometimes a board member does resign in the heat of the moment, and then recants either the same evening or later. Sometimes some board members talk to the one who stomped out of the meeting declaring his or her resignation, and ask him or her to stay on, promising to be supportive, or other members who supported him or her in the elections beg him or her to reconsider. Sometimes board members who resign have second thoughts. They may decide to withdraw, withhold, or take back their resignation— can they do that?

> **Key Point**
>
> In the heat of the moment, a lot of things can happen. Sometimes a board member will say, "I quit," but there are many things to consider as to whether a resignation is effective.

It depends on whether the resignation is effective. If it has been put into effect, there is no taking it back. If it is effective, then the question becomes: Can the remaining board members, if they elect to do so, appoint that person to fill the vacancy created on the board by his or her own resignation? The answer to that would depend on whether there was any language in the regulatory documents that prevented the reappointment of a resigned board member. There usually is not.

When analyzing whether a resignation is effective and irrevocable, one thing to do is check the regulatory documents for the association—board member resignation would normally be a subject covered in the bylaws—and the laws of the jurisdiction relating to corporations, if the association is incorporated. The bylaws may have specific language stating either that the resignation needs to be accepted to be effective, or, to the contrary, that no acceptance is necessary and the resignation is effective when it is given. Some documents say it must be given in writing, and some specify to whom or how it must be presented.

Most bylaws say that a board member continues to serve until his or her successor is elected; however, those same documents usually also say that if a board member resigns, the remaining board members may appoint a successor who would fill that board member's position for his or her remaining term. In fact, if the board is down to one person, in most jurisdictions that person may appoint directors to fill the vacant positions.

It is also very important to consider the words and actions involved in the resignation process. Perhaps the resignation is equivocal; perhaps there is a future date specified as to when the resignation will go into effect, in which case the resignation is delayed until the specified date; perhaps the board member intends to resign from an office (such as president or treasurer), rather than from the board itself. Maybe the board member was intimidated into resigning or resigned under duress. Maybe the other board members decided the board member had to resign because he or she had done something that separated himself or herself from the rest of the board, like listing his or her unit for sale or suing the board. Neither action requires a board member to resign by law, but resignation might be required in the regulatory documents. And, for many reasons, resignation might just be the right thing to do if the change the board member makes causes him or her to lose sight of what is best for the association.

Sometimes a board member says he or she wants to quit, but does not specify or submit a formal resignation. Intention may be an important factor, but the regulatory documents and the laws of the jurisdiction need to be reviewed, as they may have controlling language in regard to how the resignation should be submitted.

What happens if all board members want to resign?

If there is a possibility that all board members might resign, then serious thought needs to be given as to how to save the association from having no leadership at all. More than likely, there is law in the jurisdiction that would allow any member of the board to appoint additional directors, or any member of the association to petition the Superior

Court for a receiver to be appointed. Petitioning for a receiver might sound easy, but it is not—it requires a court petition and an attorney to help with the court processes. Such a process is more than likely an expedited court procedure. Additionally, the question usually comes up as to where the money comes from for filing fees, attorney's fees, and expenses. The banks holding the association funds will not release them to a person not serving on the board, which means that without a board, there is no way to pay the association bills.

> ### Key Point
>
> If board members resign *en masse* and do not leave or appoint successors, they could be held responsible for losses that occur due to the lack of leadership, management, and administration of the homeowners' association, especially if no one shows up to succeed them.

And while everyone is waiting for something to be done about the situation, those board members who resigned could find themselves personally responsible for any losses that occur based on their decision to leave the ship without a captain.

I am a homeowner in a twenty-unit association. Our board is unresponsive to questions, requests, etc. I feel helpless—I cannot find out about anything that is going on. What recourse do I have?

There are many reasons a board might be unresponsive. Clearly, the most obvious reason is that the directors are either afraid or secretive. But that is not always the situation. One reason might be that the board is simply not able to provide answers to all the questions. Education about homeowners' association practices is not readily available and laws are complicated. Silence is less risky than looking dumb or saying something that is incorrect. Maybe the board members do not have any people or communication skills, and maybe they just do not have ready means of communicating with owners. Especially in a self-managed association, there may be a tendency for boards to shut down if all the directors are hearing from the ranks are complaints or questions they do not know how to answer.

> **Key Point**
>
> Being uncommunicative or unresponsive is not good; however, it does not always mean that the board members are trying to ignore or hide things from you. Maybe they are just ineffective, clueless, or unable to find the solution and are waiting to get back to you.

There is also the possibility that the demands that are being made are unreasonable, offensive, or continuing, or that they have been put on the agenda for the next meeting and no one wants to address them until then. Perhaps the board is waiting for an upcoming meeting and it only seems like the board members are unresponsive because no one provides any answers outside the boardroom. Sometimes there are cases in which owners are demanding and want answers right away, and directors feel there is safety in numbers so it makes more sense to have the questions addressed by the entire board. Of course, there are boards that put off owner complaints and demands for months on end just because they do not want to deal with them or the owners who make them. Experience suggests that the demands of a particular owner do not tend to go away—on the contrary, they tend to escalate, and how quickly they escalate depends on how the owner tends to approach things. It is true that, in many cases, the squeaky wheel gets the grease.

How does one approach the board with a concern and not anger the directors?

It is better to take a pragmatic approach than to engage in shouting, meeting disruptions, threats, or retaliation. You should start by organizing your thoughts, and then prepare a reasonable and meaningful presentation. It may be face-to-face , or it may be in a letter format (e.g., email or fax). An owner who arrives

> **Key Point**
>
> Most board members need education about the very matters before them. The question is, when (if ever) will there be enough classes to reach all board members?

armed with the education and materials gathered from doing responsible homework gets more respect than someone who arrives barking complaints and orders. Recitations of laws passages or articles from research you have done can work wonders; you can help the board help you if you approach it the right way.

The best way to approach the board with demands, concerns, or ideas is to either attend the meetings and listen, learn, and show interest; or, speak directly to the board during the legally required homeowner forum time offered

> **Key Point**
>
> Being overbearing, demanding, or pushy may trigger the natural human response, which is to withdraw. That will diminish your message considerably, so avoid it.

at most board or membership meetings (required in California and some other states). If there is no homeowner forum in your association's meetings, you can submit your information in writing, and follow up if there is nothing forthcoming after the board has had an opportunity to review what you provided.

Showing interest by attending meetings would seem to be the best place to start developing a relationship with the board. Providing questions, concerns, or demands in writing may be the method most likely to generate a response and deserved accountability, especially if a board does not appear to be responsive. It is harder to ignore a piece of paper than a face-to-face request that can be dismissed with a simple *I will look into it.*

A written presentation serves several valuable purposes:

- **It tends to illustrate a more thoughtful approach.** A written presentation tends to force a person to think things through in terms of organization, structure, and message, which often presents a more cohesive and understandable demand, question, or concern.

- **It more likely assures delivery of an accurate message.** A written presentation gives the recipient of the message the opportunity to deliver it as stated by the writer to all parties that need to see it, which is much more likely to be accurate than the telephone game, which leads to paraphrasing and re-paraphrasing, which often results in an incorrect message, and which also often gets sprinkled with personal flavor as it is passed along.

- **A pragmatic written presentation of materials (usually) avoids idiocy in delivery.** A written presentation tends to (although not always) be presented in a less offensive manner than a personal affront or confrontation involving demands, because it tends to temper the emotion somewhat. When you are trying to make a point, you need a process that will allow you to think clearly. Often when people start speaking from a level of frustration, they feed off of it and the message gets skewed or lost. Who wants to look bad on paper? Spouting epithets or threats on paper or otherwise is not advisable under any circumstances, but they cannot be retracted in a written message. You can count a strike against your cause if your demands erupt into a non-cohesive rant or something more. The board will give the message less credibility—the directors may not even finish reading the message if it is offensive in nature. Dissatisfaction, complaints, and discrepancies can be noted in a non-confrontational nature. Even better, if you can offer possible solutions to the problems raised, your message may even receive praise, accolades, or a "thank you."

- **A written message gives the recipient a better opportunity to fully digest it.** Confronting board members with a complicated verbal message may cause a good portion of the message to be lost. The method of delivery plays a large part, but human capacity (or lack thereof) causes part of most messages to be lost in translation. If a board member has anything else on his or her mind when you approach him or her (a very likely scenario), your message will not receive undivided attention.

- **It creates a paper trail.** A written presentation creates a record that is hard to ignore and that tends to invite a response, even if just to avoid appearing unresponsive.

- **It leads to credibility.** If it comes down to needing credible evidence either to share with other owners you might want to enlist, an attorney with whom you might want to consult, or in seeking an objective review of a demand, a written message creates a record that speaks louder than *he said, she said*–types of testimony.

One cannot stress too much the importance of a good, solid written paper trail. It is hard to ignore if matters escalate to needing a third-party intervention—like court—to get relief for demands that are made and ignored. Hearing officers even in small claims court, should matters escalate to that point, will often ask the party with the demands if he or she has presented them to the other side in writing before coming to court. Some small claims judges will not entertain a claim if no written demand was presented before filing the complaint that started the proceeding. A party saying, *I called ten times and demanded that …* is less compelling (since there is no record of what was said other than testimony) than a well-constructed written demand providing clearly what it is you want, what the authority is that entitles you to have it, and how urgent it is that you have it, including what losses you have incurred because you did not get it.

My board is out of control—is it time for action? What can I do?

If the board is not responsive to your ideas or concerns, you may want to try and enlist the support of other owners. There is sometimes power in numbers. In many states, there are laws regulating condominiums that allow homeowner members to have access to the membership list, or at least provide a means for owners to address other members through mailings sent out by the association board, staff, or management. It is never a good idea, however, to stomp through the neighborhoods with vitriolic leaflets expressing your disdain. You may find yourself with followers if you take out a negative message about the board or management, but they may not be the kind of followers who can help you garner respect for your cause.

Here are some ideas to consider:

- Contact other owners and see if you can get others involved. Sometimes gathering support for a position or demand can prod the board into action. If you try and are still the only owner concerned, you have a real uphill battle to get the board's attention focused on your issues.

- Run for the board. Sometimes you can get on the board simply by asking—especially if there is not a full board or someone has just quit or moved. Then you will know what is happening and can have some kind of influence on the board.

> **Key Point**
>
> Taking matters into your own hands sometimes works, but it can backfire. You may be penalized for taking whatever action it is you believe is warranted, if anyone else believes it is not.

- Put your request in writing and try again to get neighbors to sign on with you in your presentation. A written message generates more accountability than a frustrated telephone call or verbal attack whenever you run into a board member out walking through the complex or swimming at the pool.

- Sometimes—although do not do this without considerable thought—you might decide to just repair whatever it is that needs fixing (if that is the crux of your complaint) and then seek reimbursement from the board. You have to be careful here. You may not receive compensation. Worse yet, you may be penalized for taking whatever action it is you believe is warranted (so get legal advice first).

Let us take a look at some real life examples of complaints.

- **"Last month and several times since then, I have asked that the board have the front sprinklers repaired. I have gotten no response. Besides not having the repair, I did not even get so much as a 'We will have the landscapers fix them next week.'"**
 Maybe the board does not feel that it needs to let every

member who reports a maintenance issue know that the work is done. The board might think fixing the problem on its own scheduled time is enough.

OR

The board may simply feel that the request should be placed on a priority list and that is good enough.

However, the squeaky wheel generally gets the grease, unless the demands rise to the level of harassment—for example, bothering board members at home, late at night, leaving messages on their answering machines, threatening them, etc. In these cases, sometimes the request gets moved to the end of the priority list as payback.

- **In April, when I listed my condo for sale, I requested three pieces of information: the last termite inspection date and the company used, whether or not our balcony doors are safety glass, and what the payoff amount for my portion of the association SBA loan is. I am at a loss as to where to go. I am concerned that this is something I could be liable for if I do not disclose to potential buyers that the board is unresponsive to requests and inquiries.**

These are questions that may or may not be deserving of an immediate answer at the time asked. Most buyers ask to have a termite report done at the time of sale so that they can get information about pests and termites. Sometimes a board may have commissioned reports on the same property already. If it does have a pest report, it should be made available to the owners.

The question about safety glass seems easy enough to answer, and the amount of payoff of an individual portion of a loan should also be available. Maybe it was the way the owner asked, or maybe the manager is waiting to provide this information at the time of an *escrow demand* (when the title company gathers papers pertinent to the sale of a unit and sends them to the escrow company). It is hard to tell. If a board does not provide pertinent information it is required to provide, there are several possible ramifications. If a sale is lost because the association had an obligation to provide information and failed to do so, there is a possible claim against the association for losing the sale that the seller (the owner in the development) could make. Pointing out this ramification may help, but it would probably be more forceful coming from an attorney rather than a layperson. On the other hand, if there is no legal obligation for a board to produce information and it fails to do so, there may not be any recourse for the owner who wants the information.

This is a time you may need legal advice from a knowledgeable practitioner in your state to assure your demands are reasonable given the association regulatory documents and the law in your state.

Chapter 6

WHAT YOU CAN AND CANNOT DO ON YOUR OWN PROPERTY

- What are some common complaints of owners?
- The neighbor's noise is intolerable. It invades my space and makes my life unbearable. What, if anything, can I do about this and other such nuisances?
- What recourse do I have against neighbors whose smoke makes sick?
- How much should I have to take with regard to creaking or squeaking beds?
- What kinds of issues can arise from pets? Is it the pet or the pet owner that is the real problem?
- Is the association allowed to set size limitations on dogs?
- Can an association make a resident remove threatening dogs from the premises?
- If the association wants to make new rules prohibiting dogs, does it have to grandfather in existing pets?
- What can I do about barking dogs?
- Children are just as much of a nuisance as dogs. Can the association ban children too?
- What is the most common complaint between upstairs-downstairs neighbors in a condominium setting?
- What are the most reliable and cost-effective ways to solve the noise problems that carry from unit to unit?
- What do most homeowners want to hear after a long day at work?
- What if I am the noisemaker; what can I do to help achieve peace of mind and freedom from the neighbors' complaints?
- What, if anything, should a board do about these noise issues?

- We recently purchased a condo. My husband drives a company truck. He has been parking in the common parking area, and we just found out that commercial vehicles are prohibited. Is this discriminatory?
- Can my association tow, boot, or disable my vehicle?
- Why are condo conversions such a source of complaints?

What are some common complaints of owners?

There are many things that owners who live in condominiums complain about. While many complaints simply reflect a lack of understanding that rules can be imposed on many things in an association, the truth is that very often the problems in condominiums arise simply because of close living conditions. Rules that cause problems among owners might be related to wind chimes, hard surface floors, dogs, cats, door slamming, stereo music, late parties, working on cars, commercial activities, motorcycles, pool use, parking, etc.

Most rules are imposed to assure that residents understand that close living conditions require highly civilized behavior and consideration for their neighbors, and, likewise, to deter thoughtlessness and disregard for their neighbors. There are many unspoken "rules" involved in condominium living that many people cannot begin to imagine, especially when the people living there have never before been involved in such densely populated living conditions, or when the people living in the condominium believe they are "king or queen of the castle."

The neighbor's noise is intolerable. It invades my space and makes my life unbearable. What, if anything, can I do about this and other such nuisances?

The young newly married couple living upstairs has too much fun in the bedroom and you cannot get a good night's sleep. You feel trapped. It is not like you can just move away. So what do you do?

Here are some suggestions:

- **Try self-help measures first.** Some neighbors will respond better to a neighbor-to-neighbor friendly greeting than to receiving a complaint through association channels. Try talking to the neighbor and asking for some neighborly cooperation, or try earplugs, white noise alternatives, air freshening devices, meditation, or whatever else may help.

- **One-time noises are different (and generally more tolerable) than an ongoing disturbance.** If the racket or nuisance is ongoing, check the association's governing documents to see if there is a prohibition on nuisances—usually there is something useful in there.

- **Again, remember—a written message is harder to ignore than a phone call or casual statement.** Write to the board and ask that the nuisance be addressed. Be sure to note that you as an owner have a right to enforce the governing documents.

- **Do not expect miracles.** Neighbor-to-neighbor problems are not always easy to resolve. People do not tend to want controversy, but that does not mean they want to give in easily or conform to what someone else wants for them. Sometimes offering a trade off of some kind will invite cooperation. The basic idea is that people want to be comfortable in their own homes. The key is to find something in common that may bring your neighbors around, or to say or do something that gives them the incentive to want to change whatever behavior or situation that is invading your *quiet enjoyment* (a legal term that refers to the ability to enjoy your home).

- **The board may act, but do not count on it.** The board may consider whether it believes there actually is a violation of the governing documents and, if so, take measures to address it. If the board finds a nuisance, it may do whatever is authorized under the governing documents, such as fining, seeking attorney assistance, and, if authorized, assessing to recover the costs, seeking a legal injunction, and so on. In the aforementioned situation it is unlikely the board would resort to expensive measures such as seeking an injunction. Even in more serious cases, if a nuisance affects only one household as opposed to a neighborhood or an entire development, it is unlikely that a drastic expenditure would be approved. That does not mean the board is without other, less drastic remedies. However, sometimes there are reasons why the board may not choose to get involved.

- **Explore your own remedies.** An owner always has a right to address a nuisance situation either as a *public nuisance* or a *private nuisance.* In addition, an owner usually has some rights to enforce the restrictions recorded on the properties. Although an owner does not really have the authority to schedule a hearing and fine another owner, or assess for costs expended to get others to comply with the documents, the owner can usually bring an action into small claims court, and ask for monetary damages and sometimes even for attorney's fees they have had to pay to write a demand letter to the neighboring owner.

- **Do not rule out the possibility of calling the police.** Incessant late-night noise or constantly barking dogs can disrupt a person's peace and lead to sleepless nights and stress illnesses.

If you have tried to work with neighbors on these kinds of issues and they continue, calling animal control or the police is an option. Sometimes you have to make them accountable by demanding that a written report be filed. If it is necessary, you may have to move to more assertive or aggressive actions to engender cooperation from the authorities or through a legal action. One thing that should help bolster your case is the "paper trail" that is created by your efforts to gain the cooperation of the owners, assistance of the association, and service from the authorities who are as responsible to residents of a condominium as they are to any other residents of the jurisdiction.

Sometimes the authorities will attempt to pawn off the responsibility for peace-disturbing or otherwise illegal activities just because you live in an association; agencies short of resources or money would sometimes prefer to defer responsibility to the homeowner's association. But you are a citizen who pays taxes and should be entitled to the same benefits that others receive.

Common daytime and family noises are probably not actionable, but if it is egregious or goes on all night (which sometimes can be captured on audio tape or via a log of activities showing unnecessary or excessive behavior), a disturbed owner might receive an award for some damages, or the *defendant* (person being sued) might get a warning. If a dog's barking is excessive, one might get a damage award, but it is more likely you would have to show that you contacted the local animal control officials first and were unable to get any relief. In legal terms, this is called *exhausting administrative remedies*.

What recourse do I have against neighbors whose smoke makes me sick?

Smoking is another thing—smoking and secondhand smoke are both hazardous to one's health. If it is coming through the ventilating system, doors, windows, or walls, the board may or may not decide to take action.

> **Key Point**
>
> Sometimes boards opt out of differences that seem to exist only between two neighbors, and not others in the development. It is a hard decision to make—whether to commit resources of the association to such a limited dispute or back out.

However, where there is smoke, there can be fire (i.e., an escalating battle) if something is not done to diffuse the issue. The battle between smokers and non-smokers rages on all over the country. But the line seems to be moving more toward protecting the non-smokers' rights than those of smokers.

Questions from nonsmokers that often arise in homeowners' associations are:

- May we ban smoking in the common areas?
- May we ban smoking in the units?

A question from smokers is:

- How can they prevent us from smoking? It's a free country!

In some localities under certain conditions, homeowners' associations can ban smoking in common areas, and there are a few cases across the country that allowed associations to ban smoking in the residents' units. There is no constitutionally based right to smoke.

One would think the seminal cases might happen in a state like California, where smoking is banned in many jurisdictions in restaurants, bars, office buildings, and public places. Legislation has been introduced (but failed before it came to fruition) that would have allowed homeowners' associations to ban smoking in the common areas and that would have allowed certain actions to be taken against association residents who allowed smoke to "waft" between walls. However, other states have been more progressive, that is, from the point of view of the courts' findings in favor of those who file complaints about secondhand smoke coming from a unit in a condominium.

Below are summaries of two court cases that took place in Boston in 2005 and Colorado in 2006 that addressed the issue of smoking.

- A jury in the Boston case found that heavy smoking was grounds for the eviction of the tenants. In 2005, Ralph Ranalli and Jonathan Saltzman of the *Boston Globe* reported that:

  In a case that tobacco law specialists say is one of the first of its kind in the nation, a Boston Housing Court jury ruled that a South Boston couple could be evicted from their rented water-view loft for heavy smoking, even though smoking was allowed in their lease. The landlord who rented the Sleeper Street unit to Erin Carey and Ted Baar ordered them out ... after neighbors complained of the smoke odors filtering into their apartments.

  The tenants, who each smoked about a pack a day and worked out of a one-bedroom unit, fought the eviction, arguing in court that the converted warehouse's shoddy construction and aging ventilation system were to blame for the wayward odors.

The landlord in the case could have written a nonsmoking clause into the lease and did not, so it took the jury to determine that the couple's heavy smoking violated a general clause in the association documents banning "any nuisance; any offensive noise, odor, or fumes; or any hazard to health."

This is a common clause in homeowners' association documents. Although the verdict is not binding in other courts, tobacco law specialists said the decision was one of the nation's first to declare smoking a nuisance serious enough to become grounds for eviction.

- In November 2006, in Golden, Colorado, a judge upheld a homeowners' association's order barring a couple from smoking in the townhouse they owned. The owners, both smokers, filed a lawsuit after their condominium association amended its regulatory documents to prohibit smoking.

  The owners argued that the homeowners' association was not being reasonable in restricting smoking inside someone's unit *and* anywhere else on the premises, including the patio and parking lot.

  The association, Heritage Hills #1 Condominium Owners Association, was responding to complaints from the neighbors who said the cigarette smoke was seeping into their units.

  The judge in the case said the "smoke and/or smoke smell" was not confined to one area, and that smoke smell "constitutes a nuisance." She noted that under the condominium declarations,

> **Key Point**
>
> Litigation activity over smoking in one state is not binding in any other state's court or in other jurisdictions. However, these cases indicate a not-so-surprising trend of increasing intolerance for wafting smoke.

nuisances are not allowed. This kind of litigation activity across the country, although not binding in any court in other jurisdictions, indicates a not-so-surprising trend.

Thus, when a secondhand smoke issue arises, either the board or the complaining owner or resident would seem to have a right to make a request or demand that a smoker at least utilize an air-freshening system. The person who is the smoker should take preventative measures to ensure that his or her smoke or smoke smell is confined to the unit, if smoking is allowed or not directly addressed in the lease.

It is more drastic and more difficult for a board or neighbor to make a demand preventing someone from smoking in his or her own home, but it is obviously not out of the question. If there is a way to isolate systems so that the smoking fallout is minimized, it may be worth exploring. If the smoking takes place outside the unit and the wafting air prevents a neighbor's enjoyment of his or her own deck or balcony upstairs, the board or an owner might find that an actionable nuisance. The same could be the case for inside-the-unit wafting smoke, so finding some method of containing it should be of the utmost importance to resident smokers. Others should not have to suffer at their hands.

> **Key Point**
>
> Since secondhand smoke is a health hazard, finding some method of containing it should be of the utmost importance to resident smokers. Others should not have to suffer at their hands.

If the board does not act on a smoking issue, an owner or resident has individual options. You can use small claims court as a venue and try to get a damages award and an order from the judge or hearing officer that the smoke needs to be contained. The appellate case in Colorado in which a judge ordered the owners that they had to stop smoking on the premises is a telling case. Even if it is appealed (the time had not run out by the time this book was completed), it will bolster other such cases. It is not out of the question to assume that this sort of court treatment of smokers could "filter" into other states.

How much should I have to take with regard to creaking or squeaking beds?

With regard to bedroom noise wafting through the walls from one condominium to another, there are not likely to be any appellate cases (binding or persuasive to any jurisdictions) disposing of such complaints. Why is that? It is because the topic is embarrassing for most to talk about. Whether your perspective is that of the complaining resident, the perpetrator(s), or the board members, no one likely wants to go to court over it. And, while the issue of noise has not yet been proven to be as hazardous as secondhand smoke, it is still not entirely free of health issue connotations.

In any event, here are some rather creative suggestions for disturbed neighbors.

- If it is a creaking or squeaking bed, a gift of one can of WD–40 might do the trick. It could be offered either anonymously, with a nice note left just outside the neighbor's door suggesting they may want to "oil the bed springs (an intended pun)," or perhaps by knocking on the neighbor's door, tendering it as a neighborly gift and hoping they have a sense of humor. Just the suggestion of you hearing them might minimize the disturbances in the future.

- If it is a roving bed, offer up casters. If it is certain other noises that should remain in the bedroom that are bothering you, and open windows are the problem, ask the neighbors to get a ceiling fan or air conditioner (if allowed by the governing documents), or get one for yourself. You could even try a "wave machine" in hopes of achieving the white noise effect.

- If it is intolerable and the neighbors refuse to do anything to correct it, then more drastic measures may be in order. You might try this: audio-tape the noise and file a small claims complaint, and then take the tape to court. See if you can play it as part of your case. That should get someone's attention!

> ### Key Point
> If intolerable noise is a problem and the perpetrators will not do anything about it, you might try embarrassing them in small claims court with an audio-tape (asking for nuisance damages of a dollar—just to make a point). However, it may backfire—you may be accused of illegal taping. It may be best just to plead your case.

Nuisances that are really unbearable may well get the attention of a small claims judge or referee, but be prepared—if you do not get any relief through asking the board or pursuing it yourself in small claims court, maybe it is a case in which you have to "suck it up" or put your home on the market. Beware of the possibility of pushing your way into a lawsuit that ends up in a higher court than small claims, and finding yourself left with—in the worst-case scenario—having to pay your attorney, the other party's attorney, and being stuck with an undeniable nuisance (by your own admission in court papers) that may need to be disclosed to future purchasers.

What kinds of issues can arise from pets? Is it the pet or the pet owner that is the real problem?

Many a board member has had one problem or another brought to his or her doorstep relating to pets. Often, the question really is whether the pet is the problem, or if it is really the person who owns the pet that is the problem. It is true that many pets resemble their owners—or is it really the reverse and that the pet owner might have taken on the personality of the pet? Try to reason away a problem relating to a threatening pitbull or rottweiler, and you will see for yourself what this question is all about.

In many cases, you are likely to find that it is the pet owner that is the real problem rather than the pet itself. If you have to deal with a barking or threatening dog, or even an over-friendly but also overbearing and oversized dog in the complex, and it is running toward you with gusto, in a gesture that is difficult to sort out until you are face-to-face with the dog, you will think twice about whether dogs should be off-leash. Pet owners do dumb things sometimes. They leave their pets outside on balconies and in patios, even on the hottest of days. Or, alternatively, they coup their pets up inside the house all day and night, sometimes even for long weekends. Some let their pets run loose in the common area, not really caring if everyone else in the development does not love their pet the way they do. Sometimes they use their pet as a threat. Sometimes, they are in denial about the problems. Let's face it—we are not talking about pets in general, but specifically dogs. Few cats, for example, have been seen as a threat of the same magnitude to personal safety, or peace and quiet, as dogs.

> **Key Point**
>
> Is the real problem the pet, or the pet owner? It might help to figure this out at the outset. The dog might be more responsible than its owner, in which case it may be a real uphill battle.

There is no intent here to pick on dogs. Cats can cause problems too. Left to roam, they can pee in the bushes and poop in the flower pots or in the sand piles where the toddlers play. Like dogs, they can dig up plants or leave waste and yellow spots in the grass. They can leave tracks across car windows, which really infuriates some people, and get into fights in the middle of the day or night. They can attract feral cats, as well as other rodents or night-time pests, such as raccoons or opossums, who like to come out and eat cat food left outside by well-meaning cat lovers.

And then there are birds. Have you ever lived next to a condominium housing cockatiels or parrots that like to whistle or talk at five o'clock in the morning? Music to the neighbor's ears? Not likely!

There are a number of questions the board might ask when faced with a pet problem.

These are some of the most common situations that seem to arise in regard to pet issues:

- **The problem may be the type of pet.** Many people are afraid of snakes and reptiles of any kind or variety. The very idea that one is living as a pet next door can cause the weak of heart to sweat. Snakes that get loose scare the heck out of people—especially those pythons that love to wrap around you and squeeze the breath right out of you, which some people see simply as cuddly. Little potbelly piglets, which were the rage as we all saw in the last decade, grow to be big, fat, and hairy pigs. One person's idea of cute may well be another person's idea of scary.

- **The problem may be the person who owns the pet.** Sometimes it is a board member who thinks he or she is the only person in the development who should own a house full of pets. Other times it might be a threatening bully who owns a pitbull and walks the streets with it, offering a menacing presence. Sometimes it is a 90-pound girl who lets herself be dragged around by her 120-pound rottweiler. Sometimes it is someone who does not hear his or her pet barking in the middle of the night, making you wonder if he or she is deaf, or simply discourteous.

- **The problem may be another animal lover in the community.** The person who causes the problem may not necessarily be a pet owner, either. Sometimes it is the person who thinks he or she is doing a favor to the animals when they overfeed the ducks in the pond and it results in a bunch of rogue ducks that do not want to leave. Sometimes the problem is the squirrel lover who puts out nuts and seeds for the squirrels, and does not realize the squirrel droppings draw rats. Sometimes it is the little old lady who leaves food out for the baby bears, forgetting that the food also attracts the mamas and papas. Sometimes it is someone who cannot turn away a stray cat, and feeds the neighborhood, attracting feral cats or vermin.

- **Sometimes the problem is a tenant.** Sometimes the problem is that the resident is a tenant instead of an owner. This can make a difference in many ways, because there is a common perception that tenants do not act the same as owners. Sometimes, but certainly not always, tenants have less respect for property owned by others. There was a California study commissioned by the Department of Real Estate back in 1985 that included findings indicating that homeowners' associations with a high percentage of renters tend to have more problems than those with a high percentage of residents.

  Many people think that tenants do not fit into the neighborhood as well as an owner would, or do not treat the home that they lease the same way as an owner would. Sometimes it is the way other people treat the tenants that makes them act differently than they would otherwise, because they feel the need to prove something. The remedies of a tenant are different than those of an owner, and because of this the association will generally want to proceed and deal with an owner, even when the animal or pet belongs to the owner's tenant.

Here are some specific scenarios and commentary on how some of the aforementioned problems were resolved.

Board member raises birds and converts condo into aviary. Some love the sweet sound of a room full of song birds while others simply find it a nuisance. In one particular situation, a board member was raising birds in her unit and the noise was driving her neighbor crazy. Of course, this had to be one of those situations in which the board treated everyone else in the association as serfs, and otherwise attempted to uphold a ban on pets. Birds and fish were generally allowed, pursuant the regulatory documents, but not in the numbers or at the noise level kept by the board president. One might assume or at least suspect that living conditions and the smell were probably as bad as the noise.

> **Key Point**
> One of the worst things a board can do is set a bad example by tolerating a board member's violations when trying to enforce similar situations in the cases of the other owners.

So, what should the board do—appease the president (whom no one wants to quit the position), or side with the neighbor who has been a long-time complainer about many things?

One of the worst things a board can do is set a bad example and tolerate a board member's indiscretions when trying to enforce similar situations in the cases of the other owners. In this case, the board member should get rid of all but one or two of the birds (at the most), or contain the noise another way. The regulatory documents more than likely do not allow numerous pets that cause a disturbance of any kind, and the board should not be allowing exceptions, especially for its members.

A board that lets itself get into these circumstances is asking for trouble. For years, the number one highest and by far most popular source of D&O (Directors and Officers) liability insurance claims, according to the national company Chubb, was inconsistent treatment of owners, meaning the placement of the interests of one individual or group above the interests of another individual or group.

A board in this scenario will have considerable difficulty enforcing the rules with regard to nuisance (or any other subject for that matter), when the members can refer back to a situation in which the board tolerated the nuisance in the case of a board member.

Another instance in which a board member's actions came into conflict with the rules set down by the board came about in the course of a document reinstatement project. The board of directors was adamant about limiting the number of pets any particular owner could have, because pets had become a problem in the association. The board president, however, loved cats; she had two cats of her own; one cat she was keeping for a friend; and, one cat that came to her door every day looking for food, which she could not bear to send away hungry. The board wanted to limit the number of pets to two, and the president adamantly took the position that she had only two cats, while in effect she was actually harboring four cats. An attorney helping with a project like a document reinstatement cannot except a member's disregard for the rules, even if the member happens to be president, while trying to lay out the rules for the rest of the association.

Feeding wild animals. Elderly adults love to make friends with the local wildlife, including the ducks, bears, squirrels, and varmints.

A resident's insistence on feeding the wild animals can create all sorts of problems for the neighbors. In one particular case, an elderly gentleman walked to the bench by the lake in his community every day, carrying bread crumbs in his pockets to feed the ducks. Pretty soon, he was purchasing duck food at the local feed store in small bags. After a while, he had to get a wheelbarrow to wheel in the fifty-pound bags of food that he was bringing to the waterside. The ducks were having babies and he was concerned that the babies would die. This became his life. However, over a period of time, the beautiful pond turned into an eyesore, and then a real health and safety hazard because of all the duck droppings. After a while, the ducks started breeding ducks that became rogue ducks, and would not leave the pond at the end of the season.

The man involved in this situation was elderly and senile, and probably suffering from dementia as well—not a good candidate with whom you could attempt to reason, and definitely not a prime defendant against whom you would want to sling heavy arrows in court. In fact, he was not even the kind of defendant who would be likely to understand a court order against feeding the ducks, if one were issued.

This is an example of the type of problem that needs to be nipped in the bud before it escalates into a gaggle of rogue geese. In the early stages, perhaps the board could have enlisted the help of neighbors to divert the man's attention, or provide him with some other activities. Perhaps it would have been possible to educate him on the fallacy that feeding the wild duck and geese babies was helping them. Perhaps signs needed to be posted prohibiting feeding the birds. Maybe the board needed to consider threatening fines, reimbursement assessments, banning him from the lake, or threatening court action.

If he could not be reasoned with, maybe there was someone in his family who might have been able to help. In communities housing the elderly, finding out who the seniors' children are and contacting them might help. Sometimes, the mere suggestion or threat that the person who is causing the problem may end up responsible for the costs of cleanup, fines, possible reimbursement of costs, and legal fees might get the attention of the heirs. Adult children or friends will sometimes step in and assist with the elderly. Short of that, the board certainly has a challenge to overcome.

> **Key Point**
>
> There is a solution for every problem, but sometimes you have to get really creative, stand firm, and be realistic and diligent in your search to find the right solution.

The other half of the problem in the situation was figuring out how to get rid of the rogue birds. The recommendation was to contact the local wildlife authorities to try to find out how to rid a place like the association of rogue ducks. The authorities proposed a plan—it was costly, but it had to be done, and it was. The relatives stepped in and moved the man out of the housing development.

> **Key Point**
>
> Size really does matter if there is a rule on it.

Is the association allowed to set size limitations on dogs?

Associations probably have the right to set rules regarding the size of pets, through the regulatory documents (which usually require owner approval if amended) or board-determined rules (which can usually be determined without owner approval, assuming the authority is in one of the recorded or regulatory base documents of the association or in the law of the jurisdiction). In all states, there are federal laws that protect people with disabilities, and they normally are entitled to have a service dog if there is a nexus between the disability and the pet. Some other states also allow for a companion pet if a disability (including depression) is noted. However, in all cases, the law allows for reasonable rules.

The question of course, is, what is reasonable? In some states the association has to prove the rule is reasonable if it is challenged, and in others, the owner has to prove the rule is unreasonable to avoid having to follow it. Therefore, whether an association can sustain a challenge to a pet-size rule may depend on the ability of the association to prove it makes sense. In all cases, associations would be expected to enforce such a rule consistently—not just against non-board members or the friends of non-board members. Some courts might even expect that an association would have in place a way to monitor pet weight, such as an annual weigh-in at the clubhouse or an owner's provision of a veterinarian's note. Such a rule should not be imposed to target a specific pet because, chances are, if the pet the rule was targeted at was already in the development by the time the rule on size limitation was determined and put in place, the association probably would be expected to grandfather in that pet.

Pet weight limits can be difficult to define. What if, in an association where the pet weight limit is twenty-five pounds, a pet that is less than twenty-five pounds gets fat in its old age and tops the scales over twenty-five pounds at some point—should the board let it stay? What if the dog next door weighs twenty-six pounds, but the owner says the dog is on a diet—does it have to go? Why is a weight limit even being imposed? You might think size should not matter since boards can address pet problems with conduct, barking, and aggressive behaviors with other rules. What if the size limit is related to a requirement that pets have to be carried by the owner to and from the unit in a carrier, such as might be the case in a high-rise condominium that is trying to avoid problems with pet dander in the halls and elevators? Care has to be taken in considering what rules make sense, or they will become very hard to enforce.

Can an association make a resident remove threatening dogs from the premises?

As previously mentioned, many boards are faced with specific situations involving problems related to threatening dogs. Most regulatory documents have some kind of provisions against nuisances and allow some kinds of remedies for dealing with problem pets. Some practitioners looking for solutions to the dilemma relating to threatening dogs suggest that the nature of the risk exposure warrants prohibitions on various breeds of dogs from the development. There are eleven breeds (at the time this book was published) that have been identified by some insurance companies to be aggressive breeds, and deemed uninsurable.

The mere presence of aggressive dogs (especially when owned by persons in denial about their pets' tendencies) seems to breed problems that often land in the association's lap. Boards have to be careful when dealing with threatening dog situations, especially in a densely populated condominium project where the association is generally expected to exert more control over conduct. In one particularly difficult case in which a board received complaints about an aggressive dog, the association notified the owner, held a hearing, and pointedly required the owner to keep the dog inside, threatening fines if the owner did not comply. The owner complied for a while, and then started chaining the dog on his stoop. The board did not address this. One day, a neighbor girl wandered over into the yard, tried to take the pig's ear that the dog was chewing away from the dog, and was attacked. The association was sued.

In another situation, two dachshunds were allowed off their leashes by their owner in the association courtyard on more than one occasion. Residents complained. There were restrictions requiring dogs to be kept on a short leash, but the owner of the dogs claimed the little dogs would not hurt anyone. The board did nothing about it, as the board members had other, more pressing problems to deal with. In an incident on one such occasion that the dachshunds were off their leashes, another resident was out walking her much larger dog on a leash. Her dog got into an altercation with the two off-leash dogs, and she was yanked off of her feet by her dog and was dragged across the sidewalk, had to have several stitches in her face, and sued the association.

In yet another situation, an association that had adopted weight limits was asked to ban a large dog that belonged to the girlfriend of the former president of the association, who had held the position for many years. This dog exceeded the weight and size limits, barked incessantly, and presented a general nuisance. The former board president claimed that since the girlfriend only *visited* him, the dog technically did not *live* in the complex with him, and therefore was not considered a resident dog, and the board could not order him to get rid of it. The association had a very difficult time with this situation. The neighboring couple, one of which was on the board and who were both highway patrol officers, were accosted on several different mornings when leaving their home. On the way to get in their car, the dog would come bounding out of the house next door, right through the hole in the screen door, barking and growling, and approaching them aggressively. The woman who owned the dog would struggle to drag it back inside, but on one occasion she did not come outside soon enough, and one of the highway patrol officers shot the dog. Again, the association got sued.

Dog problems can lead to big problems for an association.

Lawsuits can result when people ignore the rules and boards are ineffective or too slow to act.

If the association wants to make new rules prohibiting dogs, does it have to grandfather in existing pets?

If a board is going to consider adopting rules such as weight and height limitations, breed limitations, etc., and people in the development already have pets that would be in violation of those rules, the board will likely have to consider *grandfathering* the pets. This is based more or less on the theory that a board cannot adopt rules that would, in effect, make owners get rid of their existing pets. Sometimes if a board is stepping in to enforce a pet rule that has been in existence for a long time, such as a one- or two-pet limit, but that has not been enforced in recent years, it may take the position that those people who have had more than the stated number of pets for the past year or more can keep the pets until the pets die. After their pets die, however, the owners will not be allowed to replace the extras, but rather must adhere to the pet limit and not add excess pets. Grandfathering is a fairly common way of dealing with situations that would become violations simply by virtue of new rules. What grandfathering means, basically, is that people who already have pets that would otherwise violate the rules can keep them until they are gone. Then, they cannot replace them, except in excess to the limits or rules established.

Do not be surprised if the board, after passing a rule that leads to the grandfathering of some pets, adopts a registration requirement for pets that need to be grandfathered. Otherwise, what happens is that some owners attempt to replace the previously grandfathered pets with like pets, giving them the same names as their prior pets, and trying to introduce them as the same pet (even when the life of the pet far exceeds any reasonable number of years for that particular animal or breed of animal). This replacement pet is sometimes known as the "perpetual pet."

What can I do about barking dogs?

Barking dogs can be very disruptive and a nuisance. Owners with barking dogs should be willing to take steps to keep the dogs quiet. One option for owners is to use a quieting device like a muzzle, while sometimes it is just a matter of putting the dog in or letting the dog out of the house. The problem as it often arises, however, is that the dogs bark when the owners are not home. Thus, the owners do not have to listen to the dogs, and sometimes do not believe that cute little Fluffy was barking all day.

For desperate victims of barking dogs, there are devices that can help in some cases. The claim of such devices is that when a dog within a certain range starts barking, you can emit, electronically, a piercing noise that will quiet the dog. Keeping a log of the dates and times the dog barks continuously could add some credibility to a complaint and provide information to the dog owner about when the problem tends to occur. Sometimes it will help in finding a resolution, and if not, a person could conceivably use such a log, or even a taped sample of what they have to listen to, in small claims court on their own, without the assistance of an attorney. Likewise, a person can hire an attorney to write letters and make other threats, based on a claim of nuisance. If a neighbor has to resort to these measures to try and get some relief, it is conceivable that a judge or hearing officer will offer some help.

Children are just as much of a nuisance as dogs. Can the association ban children too?

Yes, children can be a pain too, and a dog owner may be justified in saying that children are more of a nuisance than a dog. Children, however, are different than dogs—they are a protected class in the eyes of the law, and they are exactly what swimming pools, parks, and play yards are all about.

If your association wants a dog park and there is space for it, it may work out for the owners. But if not, it is best not to expect that the association will allow dogs and other pets poolside, in the clubhouse, or roaming the greenbelts or common areas, unless, of course, they are with someone who needs their service.

Living in a close, densely populated development with pets is not easy—especially for your neighbors. As a dog owner, what are you to do? This is an all-too common case; the condominium is in an area where there is nowhere except a common area to take a dog to run or go to the bathroom in the morning, and there is no way to get in and out of the building quickly. With big dogs, this is can be especially frustrating. The pet needs to get exercise, and to do that it needs to stretch its legs outside.

And what about the neighbors? If a dog (or cat) poops or urinates in the common area, even if you pick it up or try to direct your pet to a particular plant or tree that is off the main drag, it may still be in the same area that the children in the development ride their tricycles and go to fetch a ball.

In a condominium development where there is nowhere to go other than common areas in the courtyard, around the pool and clubhouse, or the bits of green surrounding and in the cracks of the sidewalks, what does that leave for pet activities?

If residents include young couples with children, seniors who are shaky on their feet, or those with a fear of animals, what happens when they are accosted by a big dog bounding up for a friendly lick? Dog owners often feel it is okay to let their dog off the leash and assume they have control, even when the dog runs at someone.

Nothing is more annoying to a mother of a small child, an elderly resident who is terrified of dogs, or a resident who is dressed in smart business attire and not desirous of dog slurp on his or her pants or skirt than a bounding dog accompanied by an owner yelling, "It's okay—she's friendly!"

Leash laws in association regulatory documents, local animal ordinances, and municipal laws exist for a reason, which is to assure that dogs are under the control of their owners without the necessity of relying on the dog owners to assure others that they have control of their dogs.

To recap, problems with dogs in close places include:

- Dogs off their leashes can cause all sorts of problems for other people, including children, and for other animals, including cats, squirrels, etc.

- Barking and yapping is cruel and unusual punishment for neighbors who like to enjoy a quiet environment in their homes.

- Dogs that are found uninsurable by some insurance companies are identified for a reason; they can be very unpredictable, and they become threatening and dangerous without warning or provocation.

- Associations are a target for legal claims, a deep pocket easily tapped when a dog causes harm or damage to residents. Owners, including the dog owners, suffer when the association is sued.

   Think about it. Find a home for the dog that needs room to roam.

What is the most common complaint between upstairs-downstairs neighbors in a condominium setting?

Without a doubt, hands down, it is noise transmission.

"Sick of noise? Not surprising," says Broderick Perkins, a freelance journalist and executive director of *DeadlineNews.com*, an editorial content and editorial consulting firm. In an article written for *Realty Times* (**www.realtytimes.com**) entitled "Quest For Quiet," Mr. Perkins reports that:

- Noise is the number one neighborhood complaint in America's cities, as more people live in closer proximity in condominiums, apartments, homes on smaller lots, and nearby freeways and rail lines.

- Noise is the leading cause, worldwide, of disabling and irreversible hearing difficulties.

- Noise impairs sleep, affects sexual activity, degrades speech communication, reduces concentration and learning, and increases anxiety, stress, headaches, hypertension, and other risk factors for cardiovascular disease.

According to Dr. Luther Terry, former U.S. Surgeon General, excessive noise during pregnancy can even influence embryonic development.

As part of his findings in researching the dangers of noise for the Public Broadcasting System's NOVA documentary, Phil Trounstine, director of the Survey and Policy Research Institute at San Jose State University in San Jose, California, reported that *noise is not just an annoyance, it's a health hazard … . The sense of calm and serenity,*

where a person can sit at home and read, talk quietly, listen to music,
watch a child color or play with blocks, is an increasingly elusive expe-
rience, thanks to noise pollution.

Noise emanating between units and in from the outside sets the
stage for seemingly irresolvable conflicts between those who make
the noise and those next door, above, or underneath who have to live
with it. Peace and tranquility do not come easily in a densely populated condominium building, especially one that has been converted
from apartments to condominiums.

People are reproducing the theater experience in homes today with
larger screens, center and rear channels, surround sound, and other tech-
nologies that have become available to the average person. While the
point may be to keep the experience within the "home," use of this kind
of technology in a condominium unit that has shared walls, ceilings, and
floors unwittingly brings the neighbors into the experience, whether
they want to be there or not.

Likewise, the popularity of hardwood, hard surface (like marble),
and laminate flooring has created a sound transmission nightmare
for many. Is there a reasonable trade-off between protecting the
right to enhance the value of a condominium unit and the right to
live in a unit that does not reverberate when people walk across a
floor, flush a toilet, do the laundry, or wash the dishes in a dish-
washer?

It is bad enough that modern urban planning often involves
high-density housing along transportation corridors. But when the
residents move in, neighbors can be hit with a double whammy
when it comes to noise. When the outside noise meets the inside
noise, what is the worst that can happen? Broderick Perkins in his
reporting identifies an actual medical term for the pathology
caused by excessive exposure to low-frequency noise—
Vibroacoustic Disease (VAD).

What are the most reliable and cost-effective ways to solve the noise problems that carry from unit to unit?

Be quiet! Use earphones for the theater and audio systems, put speakers up on foam padded risers rather than on hard surface floors. Add carpeting or padding and rugs to traffic areas of the units. Put appliances on rubber mats or casters. Turn down the stereo and especially the bass. Stop shouting at the kids, and get an intercom system between the rooms. Move televisions and stereos away from shared walls.

One person's noise can be another person's acoustical dream— or nightmare.

Although studies indicate that work needs to be done at the construction stages to create quiet zones, and some architects, builders, and other providers are stepping up to the plate to create products that will help, the only thing that will save people living in existing and older buildings is good old-fashioned kindness and cooperation, effort and compromise, and understanding and empathy. Scary, maybe, but certainly true. All of the epithets slung through the walls and down the halls, brooms against the ceiling or wall, and "stompers" are not going to magically conform people that are unwilling or unable to change their behavior.

What do most homeowners want to hear after a long day at work?

They want to hear the sound of nothing.

If you are the victim of the noise, try some of these things that have proven in some cases to help.

- Learn to meditate, to shut out noise and concentrate, take up yoga and focus on the music and exercises, or purchase relaxation tapes and turn your complete attention and mindset to concentrating on what the yogi or breathing instructor is saying.

• Fabric is reputed to absorb sound, so use it in abundance—place it on the floors (adding carpeting or rugs and heavy pads), hang heavy drapes, and you might even add upholstery fabrics to the walls and ceiling.

• Add a headboard or full wall panel made out of plywood or some other not-too-heavy wood that is covered with foam or batting and then heavy-duty thick fabric to deaden noise between walls (and make a decorative buffer at that!).

• Since it is your wall (this might not be acceptable for a tenant in a condominium, but an owner could approve it)—nail up padded wall hangings or coverings. Using a staple gun or nails, add batting, cardboard, or foam to the wall (with decorative coverings, of course), or to the backs of book shelves, and place them along a wall between units when sound is coming from a side-by-side condominium.

• Use the white noise technique of a noise machine that duplicates nature, waves, the sound of dolphins, etc. Go to the local *feng shui* or specialty shop and purchase CDs that have songs for massage therapy settings, play classical music at a low volume, or listen to chanting. Choose something like a ceiling fan or other kind of exhaust fan as a room freshener for the monotonous buzz or whir.

• Take up an instrument; rearrange your furniture and rooms so that you can recreate the room you want to relax in, but in a different bedroom or area of the home that is the least likely to let the offensive noise in.

What if I am the noisemaker; what can I do to help achieve peace of mind and freedom from the neighbors' complaints?

> **Key Point**
>
> Keep in mind that revenge or counterattacking with retaliatory noise is *never* a productive option. It will escalate the skirmish.

First of all, you can do the same things to deaden noise coming from your unit with all of the fabric and padding ideas previously listed. If you do not want to cover up expensive hard surface flooring with carpeting that may affect the unit on resale, place good-sized area rugs with thick padding in the high-traffic areas.

You could, and definitely should, place vibration mounts, casters, rubber mats, or any other appropriate buffer materials between major appliances and a hard surface floor. You can find various options to deaden appliance noise at your local hardware or appliance store. Place foam or rubber pads under small countertop appliances, and try to use appliances that are quiet.

Whether you are the victim or the perpetrator, it is a good idea to document the efforts you have made to either live with the noise (if you are the victim), or the changes you have made to make your noise more tolerable (if you are the accused), so that if complaints continue or any kind of action is taken or meeting arranged, you can show some good faith in your own efforts to resolve or alleviate the distress.

And most importantly, keep in mind that revenge or counterattacking with retaliatory noise is *never* a productive option; it will not lead to relief in any way, shape, or form. The noise disturbances will escalate, and your heart rate and blood pressure will go up every time you are either the deliverer or the recipient of offensive noise activity.

What, if anything, should a board do about these noise issues?

To be pragmatic, a board has to determine whether there is a violation of the governing documents. Most recorded regulatory documents contain some kind of a nuisance clause that prohibits activities that disturb the quiet enjoyment of the neighbors. And a situation involving dicey noise complaints puts the board in the very difficult position of determining what constitutes reasonable nighttime noise. There may be a prohibition in the documents against having hardwood, hard surface, laminate, or tiled flooring surfaces in the traffic areas, usually including the living room and bedroom, specifically to minimize noise transmission. If someone installs the floor product without approval, there may be recourse in that area. In any event, the board's position is not an enviable one, nor is the position of the owner who lives below the creaking bed. It is really up to the owner who lives above to make a reasonable accommodation if some condition in his or her unit is causing extra noise. A resolution for a creaking bed might be as simple as a little WD-40 or bracing of some kind, which could easily be fixed by the upstairs neighbor. And sometimes the lower unit owner can help himself or herself by working with the upstairs owner, for example by asking, in the case of walking noise, for courtesies about soft or no shoes on the floors, curtailing some of the activities or changing the play areas of children, or creating a source of white noise in his or her own space.

Sometimes, as in the case of the creaking bed, ordering that the source of the noise be repaired, if the noise is a result of something being broken, is not unreasonable. The owner of the bed in the previous example argued that she did not feel the board should fine her when it was not her fault that the bed was broken (apparently it was broken by movers).

If the noise or nuisance occurs to the level of being a violation of the regulatory documents, then action can be taken against the association if it fails to act. What action and what would be considered a reasonable action would be determined by the specific circumstances as well as the standards in the jurisdiction where the noise issue occurs.

We recently purchased a condo. My husband drives a company truck. He has been parking in the common parking area, and we just found out that commercial vehicles are prohibited. Is this discriminatory?

The simple answer is, no, it is not discriminatory. People often misunderstand the term *discrimination*, which occurs when one party does something to another that violates his or her constitutional rights. These rights are identified in Constitutions, federal and state, with federal rights being consistent among Americans because of the U.S. Constitution. States may add another layer of rights through voter referendums, and so added rights vary among the state constitutions—California being one of the front-runners in identifying and protecting rights. Still, the right to park a commercial vehicle in a residential association is not a fundamental right in any constitution.

> ### Key Point
> *Discrimination* is not what occurs when someone is enforcing rules. It is what occurs when one party does something to another that violates his or her constitutional rights.

The other time the word discrimination surfaces in context with homeowners' associations, although still not technically appropriate in a legal sense, is when a board enforces a rule inconsistently among owners or imposes a restriction on one or fewer than all the owners.

Sometimes, owners are certain they are being targeted, and the natural tendency is to claim "discrimination." People tend to use the word loosely, but the correct legal cause of action in any situation where the board enforces a rule against one owner and not another would instead fall into the category of *breach of fiduciary duty* for inconsistent enforcement of the rules. This sounds like a lot of legal jargon, but it is important not to expect to have a discrimination claim when you do not. The term *breach of fiduciary duty* merely means that the association board has an obligation to manage appropriately, with an added expectation of responsibility because of the nature of managing money and property belonging to others.

In regard to possible commercial vehicle restrictions, it is very common to have restrictions in a residential homeowners' association against *commercial activities* and *commercial vehicles*. These restrictions will most likely be outlined in the documents, but the explanation may be very general. Look for a section on uses, and you will probably find some language prohibiting commercial vehicles.

Boards sometimes expand on what is or is not allowed by providing more descriptive details, such as signs, racks, ladders, size, or obtrusiveness, on what they interpret to be commercial vehicles. Many commercial vehicles do not fit very well in parking spaces, carports, or garages, and many people do not like to look at a big yellow tow truck or "The Bug Van" with a big black spider covering the entire exterior in the neighbor's driveway or street in front of their house. So it is understandable that there are restrictions on commercial vehicles in residential associations. On the other hand, since vehicles like pickup trucks are required to purchase commercial plates, some might consider them commercial vehicles. Boards have to make adjustments to allow for noncommercial vehicles like pickup trucks because many people drive them, but boards do not have to make adjustments for extremely large vehicles just because some people drive them, especially if parking in the development was not set up to accommodate the very large vehicles that are popular today. It is probable that no association is required to accommodate a Hummer, for example, if it will not fit into a parking space.

Can my association tow, boot, or disable my vehicle?

If a vehicle is parked in violation of the rules or a vehicle that is not allowed is parked in a homeowners' association development, boards usually have a number of choices of remedy. If the association has the power to fine or if state law provides the authority, the board can consider fines. The association can also consider towing the vehicle if it has the power to do so and the state statutes allow for it. Usually, as stated in either the documentary authority or the state laws, or both, an association has to give some kind of notice before towing, such as signs, letters, or warning tags. It is less likely that state law would provide the authority to boot vehicles to anyone other than the police, but if you are concerned, research your state's laws or enlist the help of an attorney. Do not assume it is a common right—in some states it is reserved specifically for local law enforcement, and excluded as an option for all others.

Why are condo conversions such a source of complaints?

Condo conversions are a common source of problems, yet the numbers seem to continue to grow. At the moment, it is a trend to convert apartments or houses to condos because a person can make a significant amount of money by converting his or her home or apartment building into separate interests and selling them as condominiums. Conversions, however, seem to breed problems.

The following are some real examples of problems people have run into with conversions.

• An individual bought a condominium converted from apartments only to learn that the pipes in all the units were shot. The solution—complete repiping of a thirty-year-old building. The cost—sky high! Right off the bat the individual was facing a huge assessment because the building had not been updated before the units were sold as condominiums.

• An owner converted his house to three condos, and sold two units to a person who bought one to live in and one as an investment to rent out. The original owner no doubt enjoyed the windfall gained from the sales, but was surprised when the new owner had control over all decisions, by virtue of the two to one ownership turnaround. He was upset that he had no say in the renter that would be placed in the other owner's investment condo. The original owner had no comprehension of the regulatory documents he had paid to have drafted that gave one vote to each unit, meaning the person who bought the two units would always hold the majority in all voting matters.

When an owner wants to convert a house or an apartment building to condominiums, he or she must consider all aspects, from the financials, maintenance, and use provisions, to restrictions on pets, signs, parking places, authority for modifications, etc. These kinds of items need to be included in the regulatory documents. If there is an even number of units or an even number of board members on either side of a vote, a decision has to be made as to how to break ties in voting.

Deferred maintenance, especially in older buildings, is also a very common problem in conversions. Know that a building that is turned over to unsuspecting owners without reconstructing old systems and without reserves is headed toward financial chaos.

A too-close living environment can be another real source of problems. In a conversion, the walls, floors, and ceilings often fall short of reasonable sound-proofing expectations and the closeness is exacerbated. Noise abounds when there are hard surface and laminate floors. Neighbors can often hear doors slamming, cupboards opening and closing, washers and dryers vibrating the floors, music and television speakers, and all the usual neighbor noises—amplified. And while a person may be able to tolerate this as a temporary situation (e.g., in apartment living), it often becomes unbearable once a person is locked in through a real estate purchase.

It pays to beware of a condominium conversion situation. Chances are you will encounter apartment living at its best or worst. You had better like your neighbors—very much.

Chapter 7

ENFORCEMENT OF THE RULES AND REGULATIONS

- My board is not following or enforcing the rules—that is not good, is it?
- My neighbors rent to the worst people time after time. They are scary, messy, and mean. They do not take care of the place. The owner is somewhere on the coast, probably drinking a margarita as we speak, and does not seem to care. What can I do?
- What should an owner expect would be a fair process for the enforcement of regulatory documents?
- Is fining fair and does it actually work?
- Which remedy is best?
- My homeowners' association has levied a fine against me because my bed creaks; can it do that?
- Does the board need to have a membership meeting to fine someone?
- What is involved in a hearing?
- Can fines be imposed for repeated infractions of the rules without holding more than one hearing?
- I do not want anyone looking in my windows. Can the board do that? Do board members have a right to know what is going on in my unit?
- Who enforces the rules and regulations in a small association or condo conversion where every owner serves on the board?
- My board has not enforced one of its rules for years and now it is getting to be a real problem. What can I do about it?
- I asked my association to post a list of sex offenders in the neighborhood to warn the residents about this problem. It refused. What is an association supposed to do with *Megan's Law*?
- What is the board to do when it discovers a board member is a convicted sex offender?
- What should an association board do upon receiving particular information about a convicted sex offender?

■ If the board finds out that a sex offender is renting a home in the community, should the association disclose to an owner that his or her tenant is on the sex offender registry?

My board is not following or enforcing the rules— that is not good, is it?

No, that is not good. The board should set a good example for the owners. There are even worse situations where a board is enforcing the rules and regulations against others when the board members are not following them. A board that did not adhere or failed to enforce association rules would be a classic case of inconsistent treatment and not smart on the part of the board members. It would subject the board to a breach of fiduciary duty claim and would be actionable in court, unless there was a good explanation for its behavior. If you cannot get the board to act properly, however, owners usually have the right to enforce the regulatory documents if the board does not, and have the right to make a legal claim against the board if it does not enforce the rules and restrictions. If any one person is not following the rules and regulations, even a board member, it affects everyone in the association.

If an owner sees that a violation is occurring, the owner can do something about it, which may be the owner's only recourse if the board does not do anything about it. To exercise your own rights, you could speak to the perpetrator, send a letter making a demand, or even sue to enforce the regulatory documents, either against a board member or any other owner. What owners are not entitled to do is schedule a hearing, fine a neighbor, or suspend membership rights, such as use of the swimming pool, laundry room, etc. Those remedies would have to be under the board's authority.

Key Point
If any one person is not following the rules and regulations, it affects everyone.

My neighbors rent to the worst people time after time. They are scary, messy, and mean. They do not take care of the place. The owner is somewhere on the coast, probably drinking a margarita as we speak, and does not seem to care. What can I do?

Some associations interact with the renters, whether it involves calling them to a hearing, calling them on the telephone, or going to visit them. Many, however, prefer to deal with the owners instead, which is usually more appropriate. Owners are responsible for their tenants, and it is difficult to get the owner's attention in a bad situation unless he or she is the person with whom the board communicates. Furthermore, the association has a legal relationship with the owners, not their tenants. Different boards handle renters in different ways. In any given situation in which the neighbors present a threat or danger, personal contact with the parties who are causing the problems is probably not advisable.

In any case, a board needs a good, strong policy for dealing with violations of the regulatory documents.

A board can strengthen its enforcement ability by adopting a formal enforcement policy that would be followed, which would include requiring written notation of violations or complaints or witness statements. The policy should set forth the procedures for addressing those complaints or violations that are noted. The policy should include procedures for giving the owners (and if the board wants

> **Key Point**
>
> A board needs a good, strong policy for dealing with violations of the regulatory documents, in any case.

to deal with them, the tenants) notice of the reported violation and the corresponding regulatory document clause that is being violated. The policy should provide for a hearing. The notice needs to meet statutory timelines and must identify disciplinary actions that might be imposed, including fines that might be considered. In order to fine an owner, there may need to be a policy on fines.

Having a "roadmap" to follow in the form of a policy should help bring some consistency and direction in addressing enforcement matters.

> **Key Point**
>
> Having a roadmap to follow in the form of a policy should help bring some consistency and direction in addressing enforcement matters.

The association's legal relationship is with the owner of a unit, so if there are any fines or costs (e.g., reimbursement assessments) to be considered, they should be considered in regard to the owners, not the tenants. The association has no standing to charge fines against the tenants. The only disciplinary action that directly affects the tenants is if the board considers suspension of membership rights.

What should an owner expect would be a fair process for the enforcement of regulatory documents?

Here is a suggestion for a process model:

- **Step 1: Complaint requirements and investigating.**

  Require all complaints to be in writing. This will minimize the occurrence of offhand or unjustified remarks or misguided expectations that mentioning a concern to a board member will trigger some kind of action.

  Unless any or all of the board members, management personnel, staff, or employees have been able to independently verify that any reported activity or complaint is a violation of the regulatory documents (such as by visual inspection or personal involvement in the particular incident or situation), when a complaint is made, the board (or its appointed representative) should investigate a complaint before communicating with the owner of the property involved. Once a complaint has been investigated and there is sufficient information to lead the board (or management, if authorized) to believe the situation reported likely exists, the next step is to determine if the problem actually violates the regulatory documents.

- **Step 2: Determining if the problem constitutes an actual violation of the regulatory documents.**
  Determine whether the violation is actually a violation of the regulatory documents and note the reference in the documents that is or may be violated. To do this, identify which portions of the regulatory documents or rules apply to your situation (allowed activities and violations are usually found in the use, maintenance, or architectural articles in the regulatory documents or the rules).

- **Step 3: Communicating with the owner or tenant.**
  If a problem is determined to be a violation, which, for example, could include nuisances or other violations, failure to perform property cleanup, or unreasonable bothering of the neighbors, then the board needs to communicate with the owner of the unit in all instances. In some instances, the board may also wish to communicate with the tenant, especially if the tenant is committing the violation. The owner should be notified of the problem by letter, so that there is written documentation in the file of the notice to take action. Certainly, the

board or management could first telephone the owner and see if he or she can take care of the matter without further necessity of a written communication, but unless all indications are that the owner will be cooperative, the idea of commencing a paper trail makes sense. Written communications engender more accountability than telephone calls, but sometimes a simple call can take care of a problem—you should not discount this possibility. If a tenant is involved, the board may also want to provide a copy of the letter to the tenant at the unit to give him or her the opportunity to cease the activity.

The first letter should be nonaccusatory, but it must point out the violation as identified, including reference to the particular section in the documents that is being violated, and should give the owner the opportunity to appear before the board. The letter should also state the nature of the disciplinary action that is being considered.

- **Step 4: Additional communication from the association.**
  If the owner does not respond, usually the board still may consider and decide whether to impose disciplinary action, such as a fine, or self-help. Before the board imposes any fines, or engages in self-help, the board needs to give the owner an opportunity to appear before the board, respond in writing, or attend a hearing. Normally the issuance of a written decision should be provided to the owner and kept in the association records. In other words, the board of directors should not (and in many states may not) impose any discipline without this minimal *fair process*.

- **Step 5: Fining the Owner.**

Before an association fines any owner, it should have adopted a schedule or policy relating to fines for violations, and should have circulated it to members so they are not taken off

> **Key Point**
>
> A board of directors should never impose any discipline without notice to the responsible party and fair processes, allowing the owner to defend him- or herself, or present his or her position.

guard. Such policies range from very simple to very complicated. The policy needs to be circulated to owners so that they know what may be imposed against them. The policy penalties need to be given as an opportunity for the member in violation to serve as a deterrent, because the real purpose of adopting and having fines and other ramifications is to inhibit policy violators, not to collect from them. Fines are not generally intended as a revenue source for an association, but if the owners do not know about them before acting (or failing to do so) they cannot effectively deter misconduct.

Once a policy or schedule of fines is circulated to the owners, then the board can consider imposing fines for violations of the governing documents. If applicable,

> **Key Point**
>
> Fines in homeowners' associations are intended to be a deterrent, not an income source for the association.

the enforcement or fine policy should state that if the board is considering a fine for the violation, it could be imposed either on a daily, weekly, monthly, or recurring basis. The letter to the owner should specifically state what the board considers a recurring fine. This is the only way that an owner will have the opportunity to fully understand the charges and discipline being considered. Fifteen days' prior notice of a hearing seems to be a fairly standard minimum. If an owner comes to the hearing and the problem is resolved, or some conditions or timelines are discussed for making good (fixing or paying reimbursement costs), whatever the agreement is that is reached should be reduced to writing and signed by the parties involved, which would be the owner (possibly the tenant if he or she is there), and the board-authorized representatives. If the decision of the board is to fine, that decision should be given to the owner in writing whether the owner does or does not show up for the hearing. The board does not have the authority to fine a tenant in most jurisdictions because the legal relationship created by the regulatory documents exists between the association and the owner rather than the tenant. The owner would have the legal relationship with the tenant.

> **Key Point**
>
> The board does not have the authority to fine a tenant in most jurisdictions because the legal relationship created by the regulatory documents exists between the association and the owner rather than between the association and the tenant.

- **Step 6: Fixing the problem and collecting remedy**

    The regulatory documents often allow the recovery of sums expended to cure a violation or for damage caused by an owner, his or her tenant or guests, or family members. They often provide for a reimbursement assessment, as well as a right of entry to the board to remedy a violation if the owner or tenant is unwilling. These entitlements might render a situation conducive to a self-help remedy, which entails the board going in and fixing the problem, and then charging the owner. As in any disciplinary action, the board usually needs to give the owner *fair process*, which means written notice and an opportunity to fix the problem or be heard by the board of directors before the remedy can be imposed. In the case of something like vandalism, where the owner might not be involved but a family member, friend, tenant, or guest might be, the board needs only to identify the perpetrators with a particular unit, and then invite the owner to attend a hearing at which the costs to clean up the vandalism will be considered for a reimbursement assessment.

Self-help remedies in which the board may want to go in and fix an existing violation should be used only in situations where there will be minimal chance of confrontation. This question often arises in the context of curing a defect that exists with a patio, deck, or outside exclusive use area, such as storage of items that should not be stored in the areas.

There is a difference between discipline in the form of a fine and the imposition of this type of a reimbursement assessment. Often, a major difference is that the law in the state or the regulatory documents does not permit associations to impose a lien or foreclose to collect fines, but does allow an association the right to impose a lien or foreclose for reimbursement assessments needed to pay for repair of damages caused by individuals. Self-help in some situations can be risky if the owner or the tenant involved is likely to be confrontational, and in those cases, if someone is sent into an area that is exclusively used by residents of the unit and there are threats of confrontation, advise the person to leave immediately.

- **Step 7: Requesting resolution through *alternative dispute resolution* (ADR).**
  In taking action to enforce the regulatory documents, before

considering such a drastic remedy as litigation (unless immediate action is necessary, such as in the case of a potentially dangerous or hazardous situation), the association (and any owner who is attempting to enforce the regulatory documents) should first try to engage the other side in alternative dispute resolution. There may be a specified procedure for this in the regulatory documents or state law. An association should not proceed to litigation without first trying an ADR process, because it is likely that the judge assigned to the case will recommend the parties try this method at some point.

- **Step 8: Litigation.**

  If none of the other remedies work, the association determines that fining or other action will only serve to delay the process, or the use of self-help will engender additional problems and the chance of a possible confrontation, then an association may proceed to litigation. Filing a lawsuit will involve preparation and filing of a complaint, seeking declarations of witnesses or people with personal knowledge about the violation, or board members having determined there is a violation and calling for a certified statement attesting to whether there was an attempt to settle matters through ADR. Once papers are prepared, they will be filed and a hearing will be requested if there is a need to seek *interim relief* before the time of trial.

  Requests for *injunctive relief* (asking the court to order something to be done or ceased) or *declaratory relief* (asking the court to interpret document provisions and their impact on the situation) are usually preferences in regard to trial time. Still, although hearings may be scheduled early for interim orders, it often takes months and sometimes even years to go to trial, and interim relief can only be obtained if the evidence and law support it. If the violation is particularly egregious, the association might want to move quickly and seek the temporary orders that would require an additional hearing within a shorter time frame.

The usual cost of pursuing a lawsuit cannot be easily estimated; however, a lawsuit asking for injunctive or declaratory relief can easily fall into a range of $10,000 to $20,000 for the more simple cases, but the fees and costs can continue upward from $50,000 to hundreds of thousands of dollars or more when the opposition is strong or the litigation is protracted.

In most enforcement cases, the risk of having to pay the other side's attorney's fees and costs, or not being able to recover the costs, is considerable. Usually, each side of the dispute, if acting on regulatory document entitlements, has a right to seek recovery of attorney's fees if the person prevails in the litigation.

These are the basic steps in proceedings for most enforcement actions.

> ### Key Point
> In most enforcement cases, the risk of having to pay the other side's attorney's fees and costs, or not being able to recover the costs, is considerable, and that often carries some weight in determining how to settle the situation.

Is fining fair and does it actually work?

Fining is a common remedy used by boards to address conduct or situations that are violations of the rules of the association. It is usually authorized by the regulatory documents, but not always, so it is important to check. The purpose of the fining authority is generally to act as a deterrent to prevent rule violations from occurring. Fining is not generally looked upon as a revenue source. If there are so many violations of rules occurring in your association that the budget is boosted by fines revenue, there is something wrong.

Perhaps stronger remedies that might have more of an effect upon stopping the violations are being overlooked.

Which remedy is best?

In most cases, trying the lesser measures first, including fining, would be better than more drastic remedies. The self-help remedy might be better, depending on the circumstances. In fact, almost any process is better than litigation, simply because the costs are so high and the time delays can exacerbate problems and widen the gap between the parties' relationship.

Reimbursement assessments—issued to pay back costs expended by the association in pursuing a violation of some kind— when properly assessed are generally easier to collect than fines because they may be collectible through the lien and nonjudicial disclosure processes (if this kind of collection is set forth as a remedy in the regulatory documents or law of the jurisdiction), while fines generally may not be collected in a nonjudicial proceeding.

The important thing is that the board follows through assertively with enforcement actions and treats people consistently; makes sure that all communications with the parties in question are reasonable, balanced, and based on factual assertions; and, makes sure that all written communications make it clear to the owners what the problem is, what is expected, when a hearing will be held, what disciplinary action is being considered, and what enforcement by any of the authorized methods is likely to be used. The following question provides more information on fining, as that is often the remedy of (first) choice.

My homeowners' association has levied a fine against me because my bed creaks; can it do that?

In most cases, before a board can impose a fine on any owner there are steps required to provide the owner with a fair opportunity to respond to charges that are made and present his or her side of the situation. The requirements may be in the state statute or in the regulatory documents. There may be other requirements such as the adoption and circulation of a fines policy, limitations on frequency and amounts, etc.

The issue of a creaking bed is really not much different than a situation in which someone in a unit below has to listen to beds moving across a hardwood floor, a headboard hitting the wall, a loud stereo, late night parties, or other activities that create a nuisance. Believe it or not, these are fairly common complaints—many condominiums and townhouses with upstairs-downstairs units do not have very good soundproofing, because owners install hard surface flooring in place of carpeting, do not put rubber casters under the bed, or simply ignore the existence of thin walls and floors. Nighttime noise is a common complaint when someone lives below a night person or an insomniac who watches TV all hours of the night. Nighttime flushing of a toilet or running of a shower can drive the neighbors below crazy. These kinds of complaints seem to be exacerbated in a condominium conversion because soundproofing seems to be minimal to nonexistent in buildings that were constructed as apartments rather than condominiums.

Does the board need to have a membership meeting to fine someone?

The board can usually make the decision on individual fines without involving the members.

Most documents allow the board to determine what disciplinary action might be imposed, but some do require members to vote on it. This is a double-edged sword, because in order to take a vote, the board would need to announce the violation to everyone. This could be embarrassing. In most cases there is provision in the law of the jurisdiction that allows for privacy of owners when things could be embarrassing, like in the possibility of getting fined.

Adopting the policy might be different. Anything that is going to affect the owners might be subject to circulation to association members before adoption, allowing the owners to comment, or it might be subject to approval of the homeowners.

What is involved in a hearing?

Sometimes a homeowner asks for a *hearing* with the hope of being exonerated from some claim he or she believes is unjust or unsubstantiated.

In different jurisdictions, owners have various options to ask for in obtaining an an audience with the board, and in many cases homeowners are entitled to address the board at any open meeting. Boards usually prefer closed meetings, however, when conducting hearings.

Some boards handle the hearings better than others. One board invited all members in for the hearings before each monthly board meeting. For a half hour to an hour (depending on the number of invitations set aside), all attendees were brought in at once, and refreshments were served while the owners were called upon one by one to defend the charges that led to the hearing notices. It was not an offensive procedure; it was a party, more or less, and everyone was in the same boat—they were there to defend themselves. It was taken seriously, but was not made out to be a big deal. Owners responded well—they gave respect to the board and did not have to be defensive. They usually were either right or wrong in their actions, and took their punishments like grownups.

In other cases, boards can be very offensive toward owners who are called to hearings. If the owners are very defensive in return, it creates a hostile atmosphere that is uncomfortable for everyone. The best hearing procedure offers a congenial greeting and introductions all around, a few words by the board president or person acting as chairperson about the charges that led to the hearing, and an uninterrupted period of time for the owner involved to respond to the charges. Then, the board usually either makes a ruling or takes the matter under submission, which means it will discuss the situation among its members at a later time when the owner is not around. Ultimately, a decision is rendered and if it is made after the meeting, it is commonly memorialized in writing. Some states require a written decision, so if one that is passed on to the owner is made at the hearing, it still may have to be memorialized. Judges have to always memorialize their findings so that there is a record of them in case of disagreements later.

Can fines be imposed for repeated infractions of the rules without holding more than one hearing?

If the conduct constitutes a continuing or recurring violation, and the association wants to consider imposing a fine for each violation as it occurs, or a daily, weekly, or monthly fine, the board should note this in all notices to the owner, discuss it at any hearing, and note it in any written decision. An owner could question whether due process was satisfied if the owner was not informed that he or she may be fined for ongoing or future conduct that occurs after a hearing.

I do not want anyone looking in my windows. Can the board do that? Do board members have a right to know what is going on in my unit?

Each state will have its own case law dictating whether and to what extent the board can peer over fences and into people's units to find out if a violation of the regulatory documents is occurring. In a leading case in California, members of the board of one association were able to see into the windows of a residence and they became aware that the resident was keeping three cats. The association had a "no pets" rule. The owner was fined for the presence of the pets; she sued the association, claiming that the board had violated her privacy by looking into her windows. The case is *Nahrstedt vs. Lakeshore Village Condominiums*. The appellate court determined that the regulatory documents were enforceable and the association could ban the pets. The decision was based on the premise that the regulatory document was given an assumption of validity and an owner could challenge the restrictions in it only if he or she could prove that the restrictions were arbitrarily enforced or against public policy. The point here is that the fact that the board had to be able to see into the unit to determine there were pets (or at least look toward the window to see a cat in it) was not repugnant to the court.

Who enforces the rules and regulations in a small association or condo conversion where every owner serves on the board?

It is difficult to figure out who is in charge of enforcement when everyone is serving on the board. In this case, the majority of the board would have to determine whether any given situation is a violation of the regulatory documents and what discipline should be imposed. The owner in question would have to abstain from voting on his or her own discipline, and everything would have to be done by majority decision. The majority would determine whether a fine is to be imposed, whether other action is to be taken, and whether litigation is to be filed.

In any case where a board determines that legal action might need to be filed, the board has to find a legal way to exclude the party against whom the legal action might be filed from the discussions about strategy. This is commonly done by having the board, by majority approval, appoint an *executive committee of the board*, consisting of all board members except for the member that is subject to being sued. Naturally, the board of directors cannot discuss any strategy to take legal action with the opposing party sitting in on the conversations. Once again, it would be important in this situation to consider adopting policies that would dictate what would happen if there were a tie vote. If there is an odd number of board members, but one is to be excluded by abstention because his or her situation is being considered, or because decisions have to be made about legal action, it can leave a board with a tie vote.

My board has not enforced one of its rules for years and now it is getting to be a real problem. What can I do about it?

Boards change character over time. Some boards become more aggressive, for example, or the level at which they enforce the documents increases or decreases. If there are restrictions that have not been enforced that the association would like to enforce, there are ways to make it happen, but proper notice must be given to the owners. Failure or lack of enforcement may give many homeowners the idea that certain conduct is acceptable, when it actually is not. The owners begin to rely on the board's inaction, which can lead

> ### Key Point
> If a rule has not been enforced in a long time and the current board changes course, the *statute of limitations* (the time limitation for bringing about the action) in your state may have some bearing. Maybe the time for enforcement has run out; either way, the statute is worth considering.

to problems later on when the board wakes up—for example, when an owner threatens to sue the board for not enforcing the restrictions.

One defense to a legal claim called *running* or *tolling* of the *statute of limitations* is dependent on the passage of time. Many legal claims eventually die, meaning that after a certain amount of time, the claim is stale and may not be pursued. In the context of the homeowners' association arena, when the board or a neighbor knows that a violation has been going on for years and has done nothing about it, it eventually loses the right to do anything at all. In order to be certain of the timing of rights, the law in the jurisdiction should be checked. There may be questions that affect this tolling that relate to the obviousness of the violation. In many cases, the timeline does not begin to run until the time of the violation discovery. Timelines may be established through the regulatory documents, case law, or the laws of the state.

Sometimes something as simple as a notice to the homeowners will suffice for reinstating the right to address a violation or a rule that has seemingly sat dormant for a while. It could say that because the board has become aware of a growing problem, or because of the passage of time, certain changes indicate more aggressive enforcement might be needed, and the board will begin more vigorous enforcement on some certain date or point in time in the future. The idea would be to give the homeowners a notice that the enforcement will begin, but also give them the opportunity to cure whatever existing violations have occurred. This process usually starts with a new policy adopted by the board to enforce a restriction, with some commentary on the reason for adopting the policy, possibly some reasons why it is now more important than ever to enforce it, and information about when enforcement would begin.

Remedies for failure to comply with the board's request to cure the violations could also be listed in such a policy; having them there may have the benefit of serving as a deterrent to continued misconduct and may encourage homeowners to begin to comply. It is often helpful to include a preamble indicating why there is a change. Here is a small example of how it might be handled:

"The regulatory documents for [association name] *contain restrictions relating to the keeping of pets. There are some restrictions that have not been vigorously enforced because the board was either not aware of them or did not have the resources to vigorously enforce them. However, because of growing problems related to pets, the board will need to be more aggressive about enforcing the rules and regulations relating to pets ... "*

You could go on and state some new rules that have been adopted, or reiterate those rules that will be enforced, making sure to provide information about enforcement dates and possible punishments for non-compliance. Some restrictions are harder to return to after sitting dormant for years and more work on the part of the board may be required.

The idea is to figure out a way to rein in the mistakes or situations where the rule was overlooked, and compensate and make the record appropriate to move forward to right the wrongs done by the inattention over a period of time.

> ### Key Point
> It may be possible to revive a rule or requirement that seems to have died if all reasonable and pragmatic steps are taken to let owners know it will be revived. You would, however, need legal assistance with this.

I asked my association to post a list of sex offenders in the neighborhood to warn the residents about this problem. It refused. What is an association supposed to do with *Megan's Law*?

These are very difficult questions. Owners look to the board to respond when a safety issue is brought to its attention, but the demands on associations continue to increase. Each year the legislatures propose complicated, technical, and service-driven regulatory laws and compliance costs increases for associations. And boards have to make decisions as to how to respond to those laws. *Megan's Law* is just one example of a law that puts an association in between a rock and a hard place. And practitioners all over the country disagree on the level of involvement a board of directors in a homeowners' association should exert as far as notice and warnings are concerned.

The public eye certainly is on associations. Many news stories are written and read about associations, most having some negative connotations. The media is also an area where association members clamor for immediate and aggressive action by their boards, but boards cannot act without considering all angles.

What is the board to do when it discovers a board member is a convicted sex offender?

Associations are getting myriad answers from attorneys on the sex offender topic. Some attorneys suggest getting aggressive and others are more conservative. The issues are complicated and numerous.

If the board finds a director is a convicted sex offender, which is a felony, and the bylaws for the association state that no convicted felons may serve on the board, the board can ask the director to step down, and if he or she does not, the board could vacate the position—but only if the bylaws contain the qualification requirement. Can the board ask him or her to move out of the complex? I would say that doing so could lead to liability, especially if the request could be perceived as harassment or a misuse of the information gleaned from *Megan's Law* lists.

Residents want action when they find out there is a sex offender in the neighborhood; some want the person evicted; some want flyers posted or circulated, warning of the danger; and, some want organized picketing. Most, however, want protection. If the home-owner's association takes action and makes an announcement about a sex offender living in the neighborhood, one thing that could happen is that members will then assume (unrealistically and unreasonably) that the HOA is responsible for protecting them. Boards do have certain responsibilities when it comes to addressing known dangerous and hazardous situations in most, if not all, cases, but they have to consider other "downsides" in these situations as well. For example, a publicly circulated memo or message could devalue the property in the HOA. The members affected may threaten the HOA with liability and losses for misuse of the information.

Those in law enforcement often advise prudence and regard for the privacy of an individual charged as a sex offender, and often ask that residents leave it up to the local police department to circulate whatever notices are appropriate. This is because they know that if convicted sex offenders are harassed and their civil rights are violated, the laws favoring the Internet lists will likely be pulled back. They also usually understand that publicly proclaiming the location of the offender and misusing the information listed on the Internet subjects the publisher of said information to severe punishment. The purpose of the list is so that individuals can go online and get information, and take steps to protect themselves if they feel the need. It is not for the public to take that information and further disseminate it or to take steps to harass the sex offenders. Anyone who promotes the harassment of a convicted sex offender could be sued. Associations fall into this category.

There are statutory penalties in some states for misuse of the Internet list. Some states are more relaxed about the consequences of use of the sex offender lists, and practitioners in these states have recommended amending the governing documents to exclude sex offenders from the development. There are many potential ramifications to doing so, but none vetted in litigation as of the time this book was written. Legal scholars and practitioners debate the pros and cons of this sort of aggressive action.

Some states are more conscious of citizens' rights than others, and have more sex offenders per capita, and so using the restrictions such as those previously stated would have further reaching ramifications and limitations on housing for sex offenders. That might not go over well with the courts, but the subject is much debated.

The following is excerpted from the California statute.

Penal Code Section 290.46(h)(1) signed into law September 24, 2004, provides for some very stiff penalties. It says: "Any person who uses information disclosed pursuant to the Internet Web site to commit a misdemeanor shall be subject to, in addition to any other penalty or fine imposed, a fine of not less than ten thousand dollars ($10,000) and not more than fifty thousand dollars ($50,000)." Subsection (2) says: "Any person who uses information disclosed pursuant to the Internet Web site to commit a felony shall be punished, by a five-year term of imprisonment in the state prison." Subsection (j)(1) says: "A person is authorized to use information disclosed pursuant to this section *only to protect a person at risk.*"

The California Attorney General's site on *Megan's Law* contains the following disclaimer, which visitors must accept before entering the website:

A person may use the information disclosed on the Attorney General's Web site only to protect a person at risk. It is a crime to use the information disclosed on the Attorney General's Internet Web site to commit a misdemeanor or felony. Unless the information is used to protect a person at risk, it is also prohibited to use any information that is disclosed pursuant to this Internet Web site for a purpose relating to health insurance, insurance, loans, credit, employment, education, scholarships, fellowships, housing, accommodations, or benefits, privileges, or services provided by any business. Misuse of the information may make the user liable for money damages or an injunction against the misuse. Before using the information disclosed on this Web site, you may want to consult with an attorney or merely suggest to others that they view the Web site for themselves.

Additionally, one has to click past the following warning to get into the site:

Legal and Illegal Uses. The information on this web site is made available solely to protect the public. Anyone who uses this information to commit a crime or to harass an offender or his or her family is subject to criminal prosecution and civil liability. Any person who is required to register pursuant to Penal Code section 290 who enters this web site is punishable by a fine not exceeding $1,000, imprisonment in a county jail not exceeding six months, or by both the fine and imprisonment. (Pen. Code, § 290.46, subd. (h)(2).)

That disclaimer page also says:

Mistaken Identities. Extreme care must be taken in the use of information because mistaken identification may occur when relying solely upon name, age, and address to identify individuals.

It is possible that information provided to the association by any owner or other source could be incorrect and result in a mistaken identity. Even if the information is correct, it is imperative to understand that information provided on the public websites identifying registered sex offenders is for limited use, and that is only to *protect a person at risk.*

You are no doubt thinking that every child in the association is at risk if there is a sex offender in the neighborhood. But that mindset may lead to liability. State law may punish persons who perpetrate harassment of offenders or their family members. If you think for one minute that all residents in an association will act rationally upon a notice that there is a sex offender in the neighborhood, think again. If there was harassment as a result, in the eyes of the law, responsibility would likely be found to begin with the republishing of the information from the list.

The California Apartment Association said it best in a 2005 alert: "… landlords are *trapped between two conflicting state laws: one prohibiting discrimination against sex offenders, and another exposing them to litigation if they fail to protect tenants from individuals known to be dangerous.*" The same could be said of homeowners' associations. Associations have been held to the same standard as landlords in some cases examining tort liability and discrimination. When the association is held to a landlord's standard of care, in regard to common areas under the association's control, it means the board has a duty to exercise due care for the residents' safety in those areas.

> **Key Point**
>
> Disclosures about sex offenders in the neighborhood can be very dicey and fraught with fallout problems, legal liability, riot-incitement, etc. A board should always get legal advice when confronted with such a question.

So what is a board to do? Some associations on the East Coast, at the advice of their legal counsel, have amended the property restrictions such that they would prevent sex offenders from living in the development. Sex offenders are not a protected class of citizens, so why not? Living in an association has been likened to "living in the same house" as other residents because of shared amenities such as recreation rooms, pool facilities, saunas, shared showers, etc. However, the jury is not "out yet" on whether these amendments are going to hold up in court. Some claim they are fraught with civil rights issues, and that these associations are inviting lawsuits based on a violation of civil rights if they restrict housing for sex offenders in this way. Other practitioners believe that the passage of such a measure would invite a false sense of security, since many offenders fail to keep the registry current or even register at all. And obviously, not all molesters are convicted sex offenders and not all convicted sex offenders are molesters. If a board is trying to enforce such a covenant, how likely is it that any investigation into a resident's criminal history will lead to a civil rights violation, a harassment claim, or an inconsistent treatment claim (see Chapter 6 for more on inconsistent treatment). Additionally, these eastern states as well as others across the country may not have the equivalent liberal protection in place for offenders that California has in the form of legislatively mandated criminal penalties for misuse of the information on the list.

What should an association board do upon receiving particular information about a convicted sex offender?

Clearly, a board can provide information to the association members reminding them that they have the option of taking steps to protect their own children and family members by checking the National Registry of Sex Offenders or the state's *Megan's Law* list (if it has one), and by searching for other suggestions on the Web. Anyone can do an Internet search on *Megan's Law* and find national and state registries. The state site is often maintained by the attorney general's office, and can be located by a Web search for the state. If an association uses this approach, it may be wise to include a disclaimer in the information it provides that says, "the association does not check this registry or publish information from it." Some landlords who do this in their leases also have a disclosure on *Megan's Law* to protect themselves. Additionally, if an association sends such a notice, it might be wise to include verbiage of the warnings using direct quotes from one of the websites (depending on which state you are in). People who have not been to the sites tend to assume that the information is there for the taking and for public use, without restrictions or reservations. Thus, if they received information about someone without going through the site, they might charge forward unaware of the consequences.

If the board finds out that a sex offender is renting a home in the community, should the association disclose to an owner that his or her tenant is on the sex offender registry?

Landlords that overtly exclude convicted sex offenders subject to registering could be sued. If the association notifies the owner that it has received a report that the tenant is a registered sex offender, the association should include information so that the owner can check the public list to verify the information for him- or herself, and should also provide a cautionary note saying that there are potential legal ramifications if the landlord misuses the information against the sex offender. If the association gives notice of the offender's presence without the disclaimer, and especially if the association encourages or demands the landlord to take action against the tenant, it could lead to liability. If the owner is not aware of the risks a landlord has if he or she excludes a registered sex offender or tries to evict him or her on demand of the association without other cause, and the landlord is then sued, he or she will surely try to pass on any liability to the association that is responsible for the demand.

The most conservative approach for an association is to stay out of the owner/tenant relationships and refrain from any action other than sending a periodic reminder (disclosure, if you will) that the list is available and that it is not the association's responsibility to either follow the list, check it, or take any action if there is a registered sex offender in the neighborhood. Use of wording indicating that the purpose of the list is for *individuals* to use to take whatever precautions the *individual* feels necessary for personal protection or protection of his or her children or family would help explain the association's position.

Chapter 8

DEALING WITH RENTERS

Are renters bad people?

There are many questions that arise in homeowners' associations relating to renters, and the perceived or real problems with renters. Some problems that are uncharacteristic of mostly owner-occupied developments are commonly found in developments with a high percentage of rentals. Some of the problems stem from the renters, some come from the landlords, and some come from the association. Some renters are just unwilling to live by any rules or keep the property in good shape. They have no stake in it—they plan to do their time and move on. However, some landlords fail to educate the renters by informing them about the association's rules. And some associations treat renters like lepers.

Many associations get good results by interacting with the renters directly. If the renter activities involve serious threats to residents, management, or the board, it makes sense to avoid personal contact and deal only with the owner. If the renter is friendly, however, then personal contact and giving the renter the opportunity to cure the violation before contacting the owner is more likely to start things off on the right foot. How do you tell whether the renter is friendly? If you have a telephone number, a phone call can be a good indication. If you get the cold shoulder, then that is a pretty good sign that more assertive communications will be necessary.

Another important thing—especially if there are a lot of violations or a persistent problem with residents ignoring the rules—is to utilize the association's enforcement policies by pursuing violations assertively and consistently, noting violations, giving the owners and the renters notice, giving the renters the opportunity to cure the problem, and then holding a hearing and setting up the fining process if the problem continues.

Can an association evict a renter?

An association does not have the right to evict renters; that is up to the landlord (owner of the property), unless the regulatory documents authorize the association to evict. Even then, it is risky for an association to take over the responsibility to evict a troublesome renter. The legal liability is increased when the association steps into the landlord's shoes voluntarily. This may not be a healthy approach for an association. Furthermore, eviction proceedings can get messy and expensive. It is best to seek legal counsel before considering this option.

Can the association suspend the rights of a renter to use the clubhouse facilities, pool, or laundry room for violations by the tenant or tenant's family or for late or nonpayment of assessments by the owner?

So long as the regulatory documents or bylaws allow for suspension of rights to use the common facilities, the rights of tenants and owners alike can be rescinded. You should also check the state laws for the jurisdiction to make sure there is not a conflicting law that prevents this action. In most cases, an association will be authorized to suspend the rights of an owner or renter to use the common areas. The grounds often include: (1) nonpayment of assessments; and, (2) any other violation of the regulatory documents, which may involve, for example, nonpayment of dues or misconduct. To suspend the rights of either party, it is likely that the regulatory documents or state law require notice to be given to the owner of the unit before the board holds a hearing to consider the matter. This would consist of giving notice to the owner of the property, in most cases, but some associations may include giving notice to tenants. However, in the case of a situation in which someone acts in a manner that is threatening the safety or well-being of others at common area such as the pool or the laundry room, it is likely that immediate suspension of rights of use would be upheld (such as in court) if the suspension was challenged, so long as a hearing or proceeding of some kind was offered to the owner of the unit to allow him or her to plead his or her case and respond to charges of misconduct soon after the suspension.

Some documents limit the suspension period to thirty days, but some specify that the duration of the suspension period may be for the period of the violation. An important thing to note, however, is that if the discipline is being used to punish a homeowner or renter for nonpayment of assessments or some unrelated violation of the documents, and he or she has no interest in using the facilities, it would not help to resolve the problem. If the party violating the rules or regulatory documents *is* interested in using the common area facilities, this remedy might help stop inappropriate conduct because it poses a meaningful threat and it is one of the few methods available that can be asserted against tenants.

Can the association fine a tenant?

The association may fine owners but does not usually have the authority to fine renters because the association does not usually have a legal relationship with the renter. (There could, however, be exceptions in the governing documents.)

Any situation involving violations of the rules or standards by renters must involve the owners—that is, unless the association communicates with the renters and they voluntarily resolve the problem. One way that associations can involve renters is to have a renter liaison to report to and work with the board. He or she does not have to be a voting member to make a difference. But having input makes renters feel like a part of the community and that their opinions are represented. If you include renters in your newcomer welcomes, allow them to come to meetings, and include them in social events, you will find that most will be good members of the community.

> **Key Point**
>
> It is critically important to treat renters just like everyone else in the association. If they are causing problems, enforce the rules just like you would in the case of an owner.

What is Section 8 housing?

The *Section 8 Housing Program* offers an opportunity for people with low income to locate and live in decent housing conditions. It gives many the hope and strength they need to pull themselves out of poverty and off of welfare, while living in a decent neighborhood. It helps many single mothers move ahead in life, while being able to offer their children housing and schooling in a safe place.

The program offers a monetary supplement (in the form of a rental subsidy) to people in need. Most of the applicants are not bad people or criminals. There are, of course, some bad apples in the program, but generally the program is positive and self-regulating.

> **Key Point**
>
> Section 8 is a program that helps people who are down on their luck or who have not had the same opportunities as others to pull themselves up and find their way into a good living arrangement for themselves and their children.

The Application Process

People who apply for Section 8 certificates or rental vouchers to be used toward their cost of housing must complete a fairly extensive application. They are subject to a screening process that is more invasive than anything most landlords can use legally. The people who apply for Section 8 often endure considerable time lapses after being placed on a waiting list, and sometimes have to wait months or years for their entitlement to come to fruition.

Those who are accepted for Section 8 housing are also subject to more ongoing scrutiny than most non-subsidized renters. Once they complete the application process and are approved and receive the entitlement, they are thereafter held to a list of standards, and if they violate those standards they are subject not only to eviction, but also to losing their entitlement. This is a very serious risk for a Section 8 applicant, and not to be taken lightly. It provides incentive for good behavior and responsible tenancy.

Section 8 Requirements: Lease Agreement and Standards of Behavior
HUD has an approved lease form that Section 8 applicants and landlords must execute that assures HUD that its minimum required standards will be met. Any of the parties can terminate the lease after one year for good cause. Prior to the expiration of the year term, the lease may be terminated for serious or repeated violations of the lease provisions or tenancy obligations under state and local law, or commission of a crime or fraud in connection with an application or entitlement. After the year is up, the landlord can terminate the lease (or refuse to renew) for something as simple as the fact that he or she can get more rent in the private market.

Section 8 renters are held to standards of compliance that do not always come into play in private lease situations. Section 8 renters must:

- identify occupants intended to live in the unit and notify HUD if there are any changes in the occupants (those leaving and any additions to the unit);

- submit to periodic inspections by Housing Authority (HA) representatives;

- avoid committing any crimes or allowing any crimes in or near the home;

- avoid selling, using, or possessing drugs, or allowing anyone in residence with them, family members, guests, or friends to sell or possess drugs on or near the premises;

- provide proof of citizenship when required, or proof of eligibility status if a legal alien; and,

- avoid being absent from the home for more than 180 days.

These activities constitute grounds sufficient to cause termination of the lease. Some constitute grounds for revocation of the subsidy (especially criminal activity, fraud, and drug use, sale, or possession).

> ### Key Point
> Section 8 leases have provisions in them that other leases do not have, and the recipients of the advantage have certain things to live up to in keeping the subsidy. Owners can add a layer of restrictions by entering into a separate agreement in addition to the Section 8 lease. Many landlords overlook this aspect and do not protect themselves sufficiently.

Landlord Rights, Obligations and Participation

It would be very helpful if HUD's lease form—or an alternate version for common interest developments (CIDs)—with homeowners' associations had a requirement that renters must follow the governing documents (which include the regulatory documents and rules), with noncompliance serving as grounds for termination of the lease. While HUD is not likely to change its lease forms to protect the associations, what landlords usually do not know is that they are entitled to have a separate lease *addendum* that contains provisions in addition to those required by HUD.

Requiring a Section 8 renter to acknowledge and adhere to the regulatory documents and rules of the association (and making failure to do so a breach of the lease) could be addressed in such an addendum to the HUD lease or in a separate agreement. This would protect the landlord and allow him or her to terminate the lease if a renter is violating the rules.

If landlords include this kind of clause, and if their renters cause disturbances that would constitute a nuisance or otherwise violate the regulatory documents or rules, the landlord has a legal remedy and will not feel paralyzed by the situation. When the landlord has a remedy, it makes it easier to resolve the situation involving a problematic Section 8 renter.

However, in many cases in which Section 8 renters are placed in or find a home or an apartment through HUD, the landlord never actually meets the renter. The renter might end up signing with the property manager directly. When this happens, it eliminates the opportunity for the landlord to personally discuss with the renter his or her expectations and to require the additional lease provisions (in a lease addendum) that would contain the protective language.

Can I be screened, subject to rules other renters are not subject to, or evicted just because I am on Section 8 housing?

There are many negative presumptions floating around about Section 8 renters, especially, it seems, within the realm of homeowners' associations. Questions and concerns about how to control renters—

specifically *Section 8* renters—often arise. The bad reputation comes from scenarios in which issues about renters come up at programs and classes, and someone makes a statement along the lines of, "It is because of those Section 8 people."

Certainly, some associations have had bad experiences with Section 8 renters. Managers, board directors, and neighbors have, in various settings, expressed frustration with Section 8 renters, and landlords sometimes feel they are made helpless by the situation when their Section 8 renters act up. Many people feel there is no remedy, which is simply not true. What is true, however, is that an association cannot treat Section 8 renters differently than other renters. HUD, as the third party in the equation, may or may not be involved in situations and communications in which violations are being addressed.

What happens if the board or association members discriminate against a Section 8 renter?

If a board treats a Section 8 tenant differently than any other tenant, a problem may arise. Whether the word *discrimination* in the constitutional sense applies depends on the circumstances.

If it is a case that involves a family with children, then familial rights might come into play, and some state constitutions forbid discriminating against a person because of his or her source of income. If an association attempts to prohibit Section 8 renters from leasing in the development by amending the regulatory documents, it may be drawing a big red target on its assets. It is not advisable, nor is it fair or legal, to restrict leasing in such a way that a segment of the population that needs and qualifies for housing is denied access.

As in any case, information and communication are the keys to success. An association can help its members by communicating helpful information about choosing renters, screening applicants, and holding renters to reasonable standards for residents in the community. Information is the key to better success in resolving issues relating to and involving all renters. A simple newsletter article educating owners who are considering leasing out their homes could help owners be better landlords. However, be extremely careful not to say anything derogatory about Section 8 renters as a group.

HUD does provide oversight of Section 8 participants. One thing that is not available in non-Section 8 rental situations is oversight by any agency. HUD is the oversight agency for Section 8 recipients. If there is a complaint, concern, or question about a Section 8 tenancy situation, the local housing authority can be contacted. However, the first question an association board should ask is whether the problem can be dealt with without going to the local housing authority. For rules violations, the board or manager should first work with the owner of the unit or the tenant, depending on association policies about working with tenants, to get compliance from the renters. If problems persist, it may be necessary to apply more pressure (e.g., calling the owner to a hearing, threatening to fine, or threatening legal action). When there are suspicions of activities that are more dangerous (i.e., appearing to be criminal or drug-related), the association's contact might be with the owner, but it might also involve contact with the police. However, one has to be very careful about accusing someone of committing a crime— in most cases it is better to report suspected criminal behavior to the police. As for contact with the owner, it is usually best to recite the activities for which complaints have been made, stated in terms such as, "Complaints have been made about [activity]," or "The board has received reports of [activity]," etc. If you confront the owner with suspicions about criminal behavior, saying, for example, "We received reports that [name] is dealing drugs," you may find the association saddled with a slander or libel lawsuit.

For particularly persistent and serious problems, the landlord or the association can contact the local housing authority and talk to a representative assigned to the geographic area. Criminal and drug activity and serious disturbances of the neighbors are grounds for termination of the lease, and for revocation of the Section 8 entitlement. Hopefully, you can get the attention you need to assure that the problem is reasonably investigated.

Some jurisdictions require periodic inspections of Section 8 housing renters' dwellings. In other districts, the workers may wait for complaints. Some representatives are extremely backlogged. Written requests tend to engender more accountability. The same is true for communications with the owner.

Section 8 renters are subject to standardized conditions not present in other situations.

The housing authority has a standardized list of conditions that is used for Section 8 housing fund recipients. The standards provide information for those in and outside the program, including those who have complaints, as to what the housing authority can enforce.

For example, the Section 8 applicant must state who will be living in the unit. The entitlement is based on criteria including that information. If an association representative, or neighbors who complain, have information on who is living in the unit and can somehow verify that information (through visual testimony, pictures, etc.), it may be helpful to the housing authority if it is determined that more or different people are living in the unit than the applicant identified. Another requirement is that no illegal activity may occur in the unit. If a complaint is made to the association about illegal activity, and it can be documented through police reports, visual testimony, pictures, or other types of demonstrative evidence, that information would also be helpful to the housing authority. Keep in mind that the housing authority has the right to seek termination of entitlement to the program. However, to use such a drastic remedy, the agency would need the same type of evidence that the association or landlord would need to take drastic actions or pursue criminal charges.

Section 8 is not a dirty word. It would be best to avoid spreading rumors about actual Section 8 renter problems and to avoid jumping to conclusions and blaming all renter problems on Section 8 housing. There are plenty of problems arising from non-Section 8 landlord renter situations.

How do lease limitation amendments work? My association recently circulated a measure for owners to vote on whether rentals could be limited to 10% of the total number of units. Is that legal?

People tend to dismiss the idea of lease and rental limitations as illegal. After all, many believe that an association cannot tell them what they can and cannot do with their property. This belief is not necessarily true, and many lease limiting provisions have been upheld by the courts, based on the premise that a person who purchases property in a common interest development with a recorded regulatory document that has provisions in it stating it can be amended, assumes the risk that it will be amended, perhaps in a way the owner does not like.

This is another area where legal practitioners may disagree, and state courts may take different approaches. In very general terms, leasing restrictions that limit the percentage or number of owners that can lease at any given time have been upheld in some state courts. Other states' higher courts have either not ruled or not published case decisions. Some courts have ruled that a 100% ban on leasing is okay for low-income housing or state-subsidized housing, with the intent to keep this type of housing available to resident owners rather than investors. The secondary mortgage market has restrictions on purchasing loans that cause the agencies to limit short-term leases, and many documents have minimum leasing times of thirty or sixty days because of those standards. On the other hand, the same group is not keen on restrictions that prohibit leasing altogether or limit the number of rentals, because if one of these agencies has a loan that is purchased and then foreclosed, the lender could find him- or herself in a situation in which he or she could not lease out the home until it is sold.

Some documents have requirements that say that after purchase and prior to leasing, any buyer has to reside in the property for at least one year before the right to lease the property *vests* (comes to fruition)—some documents even require three years. The legal arguments for and against lease limitations are all over the map. Even where prohibitions on leasing have been upheld, some courts have opined that exceptions need to be considered for hardship situations or special circumstances, which could include long illnesses, armed forces service, and the like. Some states have statutes that prohibit unreasonable restraints on an owner's rights in regard to leasing real property. In those cases, the focus may be shifted to deciding whether the restriction is a reasonable restraint.

Lease limitation provisions in documents certainly do tend to deter the leasing of units, as well as discourage purchase by investors or others who want the ability to lease their units. This is a common counterpoint to a proposed limitation.

There are many homeowners' associations that want to look at lease limitation provisions. A lease limitation provision that is carefully drafted has a good chance of surviving legal challenges if it is fair, reasonable, and the purpose is justifiable. On the other hand, the provisions might never even be challenged. Resident owners who are having trouble with tenant neighbors would welcome a limitation against renters. Having one might be enough to achieve the ultimate goal of limiting leases and rentals in a development. Investors and banks tend not to like these kinds of limitations. However, owner occupants tend to favor them if they are convinced that the provisions will discourage rentals. Many believe the more owner occupants there are, the better things will operate, and the more renters there are, the more problems there will be.

What are the advantages of a lease limitation provision?

- Lease limitation provisions tend to deter buyers with leasing in mind or first-time buyers who plan to move up and keep their first unit as an investment.

- Lease limitations appearing in documents may appeal to some lenders if the percentage of non-resident owners equals or exceeds 30–40% because the secondary lenders have some published standards that preclude them from buying loans in developments that have a higher percentage of rentals.

- Lease limitation provisions would effectively allow the board to limit the number of units leased.

- Statistics show that low-percentage rental developments have fewer problems.

- Statistics also show that property values in high-percentage rental developments tend to suffer.

What are the disadvantages of a lease limitation provision?

• The pool of possible purchasers is limited because the properties will be less appealing to investors or potential purchasers who intend to lease.

• A lease limitation provision could lead to a legal challenge by an owner who is denied the privilege of leasing his or her unit.

• Implementation of a lease limitation provision requires some extra bookkeeping and administration.

• The leasing restrictions may not appeal to lenders from the standpoint that, if they take a property back at foreclosure, they may not be able to rent it out until they can sell it, unless the language of the provision permits an exception for lenders.

What does it take to pass an amendment?

The regulatory documents probably specify a percentage needed for the approval of an amendment. Generally, you can count on opposition from those persons already leasing properties in the development, unless there is a grandfather clause that excludes those people from the limitations. Practitioners usually suggest a grandfather clause exempting those people with current leases because some legal authority exists that suggests those owners may have established some kind of vested interest that other owners do not yet have.

Some regulatory documents require lender approval in addition to membership approval. If lender approval is required, the board may get mixed opinions from the lenders. Any of these kinds of proposals are best considered after seeking legal advice. Trying to implement such provisions without it can lead to messy legal battles. In any event, if you are trying to determine if a lease limitation is valid or enforceable, contact a knowledgeable condo attorney in your state.

Chapter 9

RESOLVING ASSOCIATION ISSUES WITHOUT RESORTING TO LITIGATION

- How can I deal with difficult people?
- What can I do when my board (or a particular owner) will just not listen to reason?
- Is someone who hounds the board at meetings about the proper way to do business a problem, or is this just a measure of accountability?
- Is it possible to regulate human behavior?
- What is alternative dispute resolution, and can it work in a condominium environment?
- Which alternative dispute resolution process might be right for me?
- What are other real-life examples of ADR in action?

There are many ways to try to avoid litigation no matter what side of the issue you are on.

How can I deal with difficult people?

Difficult people are the curse of homeowners' associations. Defining them, however, can be difficult in itself. When asked to define a difficult person, almost everyone immediately focuses on one individual person he or she considers to be particularly difficult, and then bases the definition on certain characteristics that person possesses. However, the truth is that one definition works almost universally: A *difficult person* is anyone who disagrees with you. And the more vehemently he or she disagrees, the more difficult he or she is.

What can I do when my board (or a particular owner) will just not listen to reason?

First, think about why the difficult person is disagreeing with you. And remember, most people are not difficult just to be so—most have adopted that stance because of something that has happened or the way they perceive something to have happened.

Because of the fact that life involves so much positioning, you could say that it is really just one giant negotiation. So if you learn a few negotiation or mediation skills, you are ahead of the game.

If you have not learned any people skills, you may have difficulty getting through to the other side in any argument. However, by learning to listen and pay attention, and by acknowledging other peoples' rights to their own views, even those you do not agree with, you will find that you really are in control—at least of how you react to any given situation—and that you can negotiate a resolution to almost any problem. Trying to negotiate in a highly emotional reactionary stage is almost impossible.

Here are two simple tips to remember: (1) Every individual is unique and started out as an unassuming bouncing baby boy or girl; and, (2) if you treat everyone as if they are your best friend, you will be a catalyst for better behavior for those around you.

In the condo world, it is necessary to learn how to distinguish purely difficult or dangerous people from diligent, tenacious, inquisitive, or strong-willed individuals. Should type-A personalities be considered pushy or good at getting things done? If someone is having a bad day and becomes snappish, should he or she be labeled that way forever?

Be careful of labels and assumptions. In working with individuals in a homeowners' association context, it is better to stay away from labels like "difficult" or "disgruntled" because the use of these kinds of labels may lead to biased treatment of the person. Whether you are talking about homeowners, board members, vendors, or professionals who serve the association, once they get labeled as "difficult," "burned out," or "disgruntled," people might be deterred from dealing with them.

Furthermore, once a person is branded with one of these labels, there is often a subconscious resistance to giving him or her the benefit of the doubt or treating him or her consistently with other people. This is especially true in the context of board members' or managers' views of homeowners. For example, sometimes the board and manager's views and experiences will taint the perception of an attorney in a case that involves the previously labeled "difficult" person. Remember that inconsistent treatment of owners can lead to very big issues.

However, the reverse can be true as well. If you belong to a group of homeowners with a cause, and one or more of the owners in the group has dubbed any or all board members or the association manager or attorney to be unreasonably difficult, the other people in the group may believe it, even if it is not true, they have no personal experience with the person, or there is no basis in fact. The assumptions made about the board or manager then may present barriers to the homeowners' group in reaching the board or manager and actually being heard.

Even if an owner or board member deserves to be labeled as difficult, he or she must be treated reasonably and with respect to his or her position. You cannot exclude, fire, or evict a difficult owner or board member in the same manner that you might dismiss an employee or contractor who becomes unpopular or defiant. You cannot remove a homeowner from his or her position as a homeowner with a voice in the association. You might be able to get a difficult or offensive board member removed from his or her office or from the board through a campaign to do so that is accepted by the board or other owners. You might be able to get a difficult person arrested if he or she is doing something illegal, or committed if he or she is doing something crazy, but getting rid of a noisy, unhappy homeowner is a big challenge. You will have to figure out a way to deal with him or her rationally in the end, anyway—why not start the process right in the beginning?

And do not forget to ask yourself if you, in reality, are the difficult person.

Is someone who hounds the board at meetings about the proper way to do business a problem, or is this just a measure of accountability?

Owners who hound boards at board meetings are often referred to as "gadflies." Whether they are good or bad for the association depends a lot on motive, as well as their own accountability.

Gadflies
Gadflies are the people who needle the board of directors. These

people can be viewed in both a negative light and positive light. In the negative light, the person who becomes an annoyance gathers little credibility, while in the positive light, the person who can arouse board members or other homeowners out of complacency (perhaps thereby overcoming apathy) may be a real asset.

In one particular instance in which a gadfly made a positive difference, after proffering what turned out to be a notebook binder full of letters, months of speaking out at public forums, and eventual involvement of the press—which was a last-ditch effort to get the board members to pay attention—the gadfly began to positively influence budget decisions. The board put the person on the budget review committee, and several pages drafted by him were incorporated into the budget while his backup documents went into the association records. He ultimately impressed a large number of people, despite the fact that for a certain period of time, many people probably exercised a very uncomfortable level of frustration at his nitpicking. This kind of turnaround can happen in any association.

On the other hand, in one association a gadfly was dubbed the "Tree Man," because he always faced away from the board when he spoke and stood tall, arms crossed, facing the audience. He would say that he went to the meetings to speak to the members, not the board. Since many regulatory documents and some state laws require that members be given the opportunity to address the board at meetings, there is probably little the board can do when an owner uses his or her time in this manner. This gadfly may not always be taken seriously, but that does not mean he sacrifices his rights.

Consequences of Being a Gadfly

The following are ways your association might deal with you if you are considered to be a gadfly.

- You might get a project or be asked to serve on a committee.

- You might be asked to reduce your comments to writing.

- You might be restricted to a specific time for homeowner forums.

- Although you might expect it, the board is not required to respond to everything that is said on the spot.

- The board might take your materials to an expert or investigate the reported problem before giving any response.

- If you are disruptive, the board might arrange for a sergeant at arms to be present, or adjourn the meeting and reschedule for a later time.

The Value of a Homeowner Forum—It Is an All-Around Benefit
A board and an owner have a lot to be gained by holding a home-owners forum.

- It gives the owners a chance to address the board and bring their wisdom to the boardroom setting.

- It alerts the board to member concerns.

- It gives the owners a chance to air their grievances.

- It gives the board a chance to address and assess the home-owners who come to meetings, which could prove very beneficial when looking for board candidates.

- It gives the board a chance to expand its vision, and to hear new ideas or twists on old ones.

- It might be the first opportunity the board has to get a hint of a prevailing problem in regard to maintenance or other issues relating to association property that needs attention.

- It gives the board the opportunity to listen to the home-owners and acknowledge them, which is important in a healthy relationship.

Is it possible to regulate human behavior?

A nasty person often remains a nasty person, and the same goes for a crazy person. Belligerence is seldom curable. Selfish behavior is common in self-centered people. Stupidity, although it can be cured, takes a willing idiot. Homeowners' association boards are sometimes expected to be able to fix everything and act on everything that an owner wants them to act upon. They are asked to solve problems that derive from human behavior, something no one really has much control over. Of course, punishment can be meted out and rules can be adopted, which are the kinds of deterrents that work on reason-able people—but what about the rest?

If a person is harassing or threatening another person, the board may be able to get help from a knowledgeable source, such as an attorney or a police officer. These people can recommend resources that would help, for example, an individual file with the courts for a restraining order to protect him- or herself without an attorney. The police sometimes intervene; neighborhood watch officers can help groups of people cope with and work to beat crime in their neighborhoods. Sometimes member cooperation with the board in an effort to deal with a serious neighborhood situation might work better than spending the money to try and get a restraining order or other court order against people you do not even know or might not be able to get served with legal papers.

What is alternative dispute resolution, and can it work in a condominium environment?

Do not ever underestimate the value of an alternative dispute resolution (ADR) process, which could include mediation or arbitration. *Alternative dispute resolution* is a way to handle a legal case or disagreement outside of the courtroom.

Mediation is a process that involves the use of a neutral facilitator to meet with the parties, and their attorneys as well if they are involved. If the facilitator is properly trained to conduct a mediation, there is a strong likelihood of success. The following is a real-life example of a very difficult situation that illustrates that, even in the worst cases, there is a chance of settling without protracted litigation expenses through mediation.

Example: How Mediation Solved a Tough Problem for a Community and Saved Over $50,000

The park in a medium-sized homeowners' association had been overrun by scary-looking kids. Some in the community thought they were members of a gang; most of the kids seemed to hang out with the teenage sons of one particular family in the community. Their presence was quite noticeable and included parking lots littered with debris; picnic tables adorned with carved graffiti; speeding cars; ominous strangers showing up at dusk to party in the park, even though a curfew had been set. Things were so bad that board members resigned and residents began listing their homes for sale.

The residents considered their options: fining the owners—that is, the parents (who did not speak English)—or perhaps irritating them with a stream of warning letters; filing a lawsuit, which would probably touch off a long, costly, vitriolic battle; pressing criminal charges; or, living with the situation.

None of these solutions seemed right. Warning letters can create barriers to communication and exacerbate an existing problem. Lawsuits disrupt everyone's life, not to mention home sales, and can be costly. Restraining orders probably could be obtained, but only against the sons, while the non-resident strangers could keep coming and going. Accepting the situation and doing nothing was ruled out.

There are various types of alternative dispute resolutions, but in this case, *mediation* seemed to be the best route. The board and management, although hesitant because of fear of retaliation, finally agreed. A mediation was arranged finally, to be held in a meeting room at the police department. It was the only place the board was willing to meet with the family.

The board members, the parents, and the three teenage sons were brought together in the same room for the session. The proceedings were tense in the beginning. The mediation was conducted in a safe and neutral setting, with a mediator who kept control of the process and gave each of the parties a chance to explain their positions, fears, and desires.

Board members expressed their concerns first. The parents did not speak any English and so the daughter, who was also present, served as an interpreter. After about an hour, and as things seemed deadlocked, out of the blue, the youngest son spoke up, surprising everyone. As the youngest child, he said he was guilt-stricken by the difficulties that he and his older brothers were causing their parents. Their parents were not wealthy, he explained, yet they had to incur these expenses and take time off work to attend the mediation. The teenager addressed the board directly and he apologized. All parties eventually agreed to very limited uses of the park by the sons—basically, that they could not invite more than one guest each to the complex at a time, and could not take more than one guest to the park at a time, and each party agreed to pay their own attorney's fees. The agreement was signed by all of the people present. Shortly thereafter, the problem was resolved as the teenagers changed their behavior and complied with the agreement.

It has been several years now since the mediation session, and the problem never resurfaced.

The impetus for this settlement was simple: No one wanted things to proceed any further into the legal system. Legal costs for a protracted court battle could easily have cost well over $50,000. The total costs in this case were about $4,000. The cost for the mediator's services was approximately $2,000, with each side paying one-half. The additional costs were attorney's fees on both sides. ADR saved time as well—the entire process took just a few months. Legal battles can drag on for years.

Use of ADR on the Rise
It is clear that people everywhere are looking for alternatives to costly, painful, relationship-damaging court battles. Even employers these days are including binding arbitration or other ADR clauses in employment agreements.

For community associations, in which disputes often pit neighbor against neighbor, it is a tailor-made solution that often preserves the relationship. Remember the 1960s' aphorism "make love, not war"? That is not such a bad idea—especially in a homeowners' association, where people have to live together, often in close proximity, for a long, long time.

To that end, much has been written about ADR, which involves solving problems in a way other than litigation. Most states have promoted such efforts—either within the courts or, even more commonly, through special arbitration or mediation programs. In California, for example, a portion of all court-filing fees is offered to local dispute-resolution groups that apply for grants, to ensure that communities have low-cost ADR services available to would-be litigants. In addition, there are statutes that require the association and any owner who is contemplating suing the association or, in certain cases, another owner, to try and engage the other side in some form of alternative dispute resolution before litigation can even be filed. A party has to file a certificate about the attempt with any filing of litigation that qualifies.

Bad experiences with ADR are not unheard of, but still, they cannot hold a candle to bad litigation stories. ADR does not work in every instance, but given a chance, it is often less confrontational, less demanding, and more satisfying than litigation.

There is a wide range of ADR options available today. They are described as follows. Remember, too, that resolution of any single dispute can involve a combination of these processes, integrated with litigation, or taking place as required by law during litigation. Association attorneys and managers can play a large role in advising associations on whether ADR is appropriate in a specific situation, and if so, in selecting which type is best.

Types of ADR in Use Today

- **Mediation.** Perhaps the best-known and least-understood ADR process is mediation, which makes use of a neutral third party. A mediator guides disputants through a relatively informal process aimed at identifying everyone's interests and issues, and encouraging the groups to communicate with each other in a safe, confidential setting. The ultimate goal is to help the groups find their own solution.

The parties generally choose the mediator based either on a referral or on the expertise and experience of the individual; if litigation is involved, the mediator might be court-appointed. The process is confidential. In fact, the mediator will ask the parties to sign a confidentiality statement agreeing that they will not repeat what was said in the session or use the substance of the mediation discussions in court against the other party. Mediation is generally considered a nonbinding process, meaning that the parties have other options if it does not work.

Mediation is a good process to use when one party has an ongoing relationship with the other party—for example, as neighbors, family members, or employers/employees. It is among the least expensive alternatives, and one of the most successful, especially when all the parties are there voluntarily (meaning that they want to resolve the dispute). Indeed, based on recent statistics, the success rate for mediation is between 65% and 90%—lower for court-referred mediations, higher for privately convened ones. Speed is another selling point for mediation; association disputes often can be settled in three to four hours.

- **Binding arbitration.** Binding arbitration is just that—binding. An arbitration session is held, the arbitrator renders a decision, the decision is presented for court approval, and a court order makes the decision enforceable. Binding arbitration decisions are subject to judicial review only in very specific cases—if the arbitrator committed fraud, for example, or if either party was not allowed to present its case.

Some people fear that arbitrators have more power and flexibility than judges—with none of the accountability—or they feel severely limited in their choices when binding arbitration is imposed by the courts, and thus resent the process. Without question, however, binding arbitration often saves the public more money and grief than can be easily quantified. Most people do not realize that the enormous costs of protracted litigation eventually filter down to the tax-paying citizen.

Generally, the finality of binding arbitration is what makes the process so appealing. People who have been involved in trials and appeals know that a case can drag on seemingly forever, with appeal costs becoming so prohibitive that it is easier to give up.

• **Nonbinding arbitration.** Decisions rendered in nonbinding arbitration sessions are not binding, meaning if either party disagrees with the decision, it does not have to accept it. If they both agree, however, they may sign a binding agreement. Then, the proceeding that follows is binding.

You can find yourself in nonbinding arbitration because you chose it, or because you were thrust into the process by virtue of a contractual clause or a judicial mandate. Depending on the level of damages, many court cases are directed to arbitration.

Arbitration proceedings are much like trials, with a presiding party or parties—usually one arbitrator or three, with one chosen by each party, and then a third chosen by the two arbitrators—sitting to hear evidence and render a decision. But arbitration is less formal than a trial. The arbitrator usually is not always required to follow the rules of evidence, meaning that testimony, hearsay, and records that would be excluded in a trial might not be off-limits.

In choosing nonbinding arbitration, parties are generally indicating a desire for an inexpensive, quick resolution. Thus, the decision is usually advisory in nature—but it usually is a good indication of what you could expect at trial. Some consider nonbinding arbitration to be an unnecessary expense and a waste of time because there is no guaranteed resolution. Others are happy to get into a setting that will give them some true indication of where they might stand if they end up in court.

- **Hybrids of mediation and arbitration.** Sometimes it is appropriate to use both arbitration and mediation for the same case. An example is mediation/arbitration in which a neutral third party first tries to mediate the dispute, then, if that is unsuccessful, makes a decision that may or may not involve an arbitration-type proceeding.

   Arbitration/mediation is the reverse: The third party arbitrates the dispute, then seals the decision until the parties go through mediation. If the dispute is not resolved through mediation, the decision—which the parties have agreed to accept—is unsealed.

- **Negotiation.** In a negotiation, the disputing parties themselves—and in some cases their attorneys—work out a solution, through either written or phone exchanges or even face-to-face meetings. The parties have complete control over the proceedings, which can lead to a written, enforceable agreement, an oral agreement, or something as simple as a new understanding. Negotiations can be friendly or heated; it is best to try this alternative first and work with the other party until negotiations break down. For reasonable people who are able (and willing) to listen, understand, empathize, and communicate, this is often successful. The least formal and most private of the ADR processes, negotiation is also usually the least expensive, and generally promotes the most cooperative resolution.

- **Conciliation.** A conciliator is a neutral third party who helps facilitate communication during a dispute. Conciliation can produce the same sorts of agreements that are made through negotiation or mediation, with the facilitator helping the parties arrive at their own resolution. A difference between conciliation and mediation, however, is that a conciliator can be anyone the parties both or all believe is capable of helping and remaining neutral in the situation. It is often someone who simply can help the parties remain peaceful so they can discuss matters (e.g., a counselor), or someone who might make suggestions (e.g., a minister). Sometimes conciliation amounts to an agreement to settle based on the opinion of a specially chosen, expert, neutral person.

- **Moderated settlement.** This is a process under which a court orders the parties—usually fairly close to trial—to participate in a settlement conference conducted by a court-appointed judge or attorney. The nature of the conference depends heavily on the style of the person conducting it. Some judges and attorneys take a heavy-handed approach—"You are not leaving this room until you reach a settlement, even if it takes all night"—while others are more mediative, caucusing with each party and their attorneys separately.

- **Fact-finding.** A neutral third party—chosen by the disputants or court-appointed—also helps with fact-finding by gathering information about whatever issues are in question. In a homeowners' association, this process might be used to establish the facts of an enforcement case, which then might be accepted by the parties. California has a summary procedure in which the facts, if stipulated, can be submitted to the court, leaving no need for discovery or a protracted trial, and avoiding a drawn-out legal battle. This is a great example of how ADR can be coupled with a legal proceeding to save time and money.

Which alternative dispute resolution process might be right for me?

ADR is not a one-size-fits-all solution. As you can see, there are many ways to approach solving community association problems using these methods. Each circumstance is different and your attorney or manager can help guide you. If you really want to settle a dispute, you would do well to submit to mediation; however, if you just want to win, no matter what the cost, if you want to rely on your attorney, or if you want to have someone else tell you what to do, arbitration or even litigation might be for you. (After all, that is often what the latter two forums are about—choosing to give up the opportunity to make your own decisions.)

Few disputes are so all-or-nothing that there is not room for settling differences through intercessions or friendly intervention. Even the most emotionally charged situations can be resolved through means other than litigation, if the parties are given the opportunity. Our courts will always be an important and invaluable resource, but it is critical that you choose your court battles wisely and do not overlook *any* of your options.

What are other real life examples of ADR in action?

- **Arbitration.** Residents in one association complained about a swim team that had been granted use of the community's swimming pool. The board interpreted the regulatory documents as allowing the use, but when the association's attorney disagreed, the board instigated an arbitration proceeding, specifically because board members wanted a final determination. The arbitrator found that the regulatory documents did not authorize the use, and that an amendment would have to be submitted to a member vote.
- **Mediation.** One family's portable basketball hoop occasionally ended up in the street, which led to children playing in traffic. Worried about the safety hazards, the board decided that the portable unit violated association rules, and they had it removed. The family immediately reported the unit stolen and demanded that police arrest the board members. Mediation was used in this case, and everyone ultimately agreed on standards for using, maintaining, and storing basketball hoops.

- **Conciliation.** An owner withheld assessments because a leaky roof had not been repaired. The association filed a lien and threatened eviction. The owner located a legal expert online, and the board agreed to accept the opinion of the expert. The expert wrote an opinion stating the law did not allow assessments to be withheld in such cases. The owner paid the assessments immediately.

- **Mediation hybrid.** One resident, who had a serious allergy to pet dander, was bothered by the dander left behind in the common elevator. The resident who was responsible for the pet dander in the elevator had a disability that required the use of a companion dog. The manager served as facilitator in a mediation-type process and an agreement was reached. All three parties split the cost of extra vacuuming in the elevators and the hallways, and they worked out a schedule for using the elevator.

Chapter 10

WHAT CAN I DO ABOUT MY SITUATION?

- How can I approach my neighbor without starting World War III?
- Can I sue if I do not like the condo I bought?
- Is there any way out?
- The board told me to just sell my condo if I do not like living in my association, but I do not really see that as being an option. What can I do?
- What other resources can I use to educate myself on condo ownership?
- Our board hired a manager who is terrible. We are a small association and could not afford the hire in the first place. We do not want an outside manager. What are our rights as homeowners?
- We do not like the manager our board hired at all, and have told the board on numerous occasions. The board refuses to act—do we have any rights?
- We have an owner who is perfectly willing to do the books and manage the association for $200 per month—can we use that person?
- Where can I look for a trained and experienced manager?
- Where can condo owners find the right kind of legal help?

How can I approach my neighbor without starting World War III?

With regard to any neighbor-to-neighbor issue, what recourse do you have? Many people today fear confrontation. In the condominium setting, most would rather have the board fix it than talk to a neighbor.

When the problem is noise or some kind of disturbance, many would rather suffer in silence or deal with sleepless nights than rock the boat and complain to the neighbors. Most let the issues go until they are mad, tired, and not at their best. Then, instead of talking with the neighbors, they resort to using the broom handle to do the dirty work.

Experience says that this type of retaliatory ploy rarely works, and instead tends to escalate the problem. The person upstairs assumes that the person downstairs is a real jerk because he or she is not willing to knock on the door. The person downstairs assumes the person upstairs is a real jerk because the noise continues and no one comes to the door to apologize. Things just tend to go downhill from there.

Treat the Person Like He or She Is Your Best Friend, Not Your Mortal Enemy

When you zero in on whatever method you have chosen for contact, pretend the neighbor (regardless of which position you are in) is a friend, not a foe. It may take some practice in role-playing to overcome the fact that the neighbor has been doing something that has been making you angry for weeks or months. It is better to assume that he or she is a reasonable person than to assume he or she is unreasonable. You will find out how reasonable your neighbor is eventually, but at least you will have a chance at success if you begin by being the good guy who wants to solve a problem, rather than the enforcer or accuser who wants the person who has been a nuisance to you to pay.

Have Some Possible Solutions in Mind to Offer as Soon as You Get Over the First Hurdle of Greeting the Neighbor Like a Civilized Person

You can, through an attitude of helpful cooperation, possibly convince the neighbor to try some simple measures to resolve the problem. The noise perpetrator might be asked if he or she can put down a rug and some padding in traffic areas, or take some of the other measures noted in previous chapters to minimize or deaden sound. The noise victim could be asked to make a call if the noise level becomes disturbing, or leave a note, or just about anything less offensive than banging on the ceiling or wall with a broom handle. In regard to pet issues, perhaps you could suggest considering another home for some of the pets, or that a dog owner employ barking mechanisms to control barking.

What Else Can I Do to Handle the Situation if I Do Not Want to Initiate Face-to-Face Confrontation?

One thing you can do is check the state law, local ordinances (such as for noise or too many pets), building codes (such as for intrusive construction issues), and the regulatory documents including the rules for the association, and drop a copy on your neighbor's door if you find something that applies. Most regulatory documents have a prohibition against nuisances. Most, if not all, state laws prohibit nuisances, and many localities have ordinances prohibiting loud noises or too many animals.

Perhaps by enlightening your neighbor, you will solve the problem. But, maybe that is not likely. If you have never talked to your neighbor, and if you are at the broom-banging and the "I-am-so-frustrated-I-am-going-to-give-up-trying" stage, laying down the law on the doorstep does not seem the most likely way to resolve the problem. Some kind of communication has to be established. And it is of utmost importance to practice a little tact in your approach, whether it be in person, via an intermediary or messenger of some kind, or the mail.

The absolute worst thing you can do is to spill all the resentment built up over the past weeks or months of anxiety over what has been happening in the communication, whatever it is, whether you are the noisemaker or the victim of the noisemaking.

Another thing you can do is check with your local mediation group and try to arrange a mediation with your neighbors. Many states have programs that encourage mediation, and groups that receive funds that come from a portion of litigation filing fees to parcel out low- and no-cost mediation services. These groups can generally be located either through the Internet or by a telephone call to your local court administration office. Mediators can also be located through the local bar association, and many jurisdictions also have groups of retired judges who have become mediators. Mediation is a process whereby the disputants meet with a facilitator who is trained, capable, and neutral to the dispute. The facilitator can often help the parties understand each other and encourage parties to come to a session.

A third thing you can try is enlisting the help of neighbors if the problem reaches other units or escalates. If the problem reaches beyond your unit, it would be appropriate to try to enlist the help of others to get involved and make complaints to the association or the neighbor who is causing the noise. The more people that complain, the more likely it is that the board, and any hearing officer—if the matter rises to the level of a mediation or an arbitration (both of which are processes alternative to litigation) or a court process (small claims or otherwise)—will take action. If the problem escalates and the perpetrator begins to act out of spite after complaints have been made or solutions have been offered to him or her directly, this may be the way to go. There may be some safety, as well as power, in numbers.

Finally, when it comes to the time to do or die, choose the path that is most right for you. In some cases, residents simply decide that the problem is not resolvable through any affordable or reasonable channels, and they consider whether to move away. It is not as easy to move away from a nuisance in a condominium as it is in an apartment, and for this reason it is more important than ever to commit to going forward with the complaint to the end, or to resolve to let it go and learn to live with it. Either position is a difficult one to be in, but most people can tolerate a plan of action (e.g., moving in the foreseeable future) or simple acceptance better than a chaotic and ongoing futile battle with a neighbor.

Can I sue if I do not like the condo I bought? I hate the new color of the buildings, the board, the neighbors, the parking problems, and the fact that I cannot work at home. My real estate agent did not tell me about any of these things. Can I sue my real estate agent, or anyone else, for that matter?

Sure—anyone can sue anyone. This is a free country, and everyone has access to lawyers and the grandiose opportunity to sue. Owners have been known to sue Realtors. And their lawyers are often willing to help them find other defendants as well.

However, the cost to litigate is often very high. People have been known to lose everything, even their homes, pursuing a frivolous and emotion-driven lawsuit. Your decision to bring a matter to court may well be influenced by the geographics or demographics of your area. For example, the per capita number of lawsuits and per capita number of working attorneys in California is undoubtedly much higher than in Iowa or anywhere else in the Midwest and central states. And logically, there may be more attorneys readily available to take your case if you find yourself in a situation with an attorney you do not like. The cost to bring a lawsuit, however, is high no matter what state you are in. Trying to get out of a real estate contract does not suggest a type of action that is commonly taken *on retainer* (meaning the attorney assumes the cost and risk of success, receiving in return a portion of a monetary judgment or an attorney's fees award). And of course, the million-dollar question is if there is a viable defense to your not knowing what you wish you had known. Should you have known what you were getting into? Should you have investigated? Should you have read more of the available materials? Asked for legal advice? Asked more questions?

There was a case in New Jersey where a real estate agent for the seller advertised that pets were welcome. It happened that the regulatory documents did not allow dogs, but did allow cats. The purchasers of a condominium in the development refused to give up their two chihuahuas and sued the Realtors involved in the transaction for failure to disclose that there were no dogs allowed. At the time this book was published, the case was still undecided; however, you can see that when a purchaser becomes unhappy with a transaction, he or she is going to look for someone to compensate for his or her discomfort.

Owners have been known to sue the seller of a condominium. There have undoubtedly been many lawsuits throughout the nation where purchasers have sued for damages or to get a sales contract rescinded because they did not get what they thought they were getting in the transaction. All it takes is bad news, say, of a big special assessment coming down the pike, for a recent purchaser to answer his or her intuition and take action to get out of the association while it is still early enough to manage.

Last but not least, buyers have been known to sue their homeowners' associations if they are unhappy with their purchase. There was a seminal case in California where a purchaser sued the association for failure to disclose a drainage/maintenance issue related to the property purchased. The purchaser was not successful—the court determined that the purchaser's legal relationship was with the seller, and not the homeowners' association. In other words, a purchaser should not look to a homeowners' association to make disclosures related to the sale of a *separate interest*. However, that does not mean that every association is completely off the hook in this kind of situation; if the seller believes the association failed in its disclosure obligations, he or she could turn around and sue the association as part of the same legal action.

Again, bad news in homeowners' associations can trigger certain reactions that might extend to lawsuits. Often, the bigger the financial loss to the *plaintiff* (suing party), the farther the plaintiff's lawyer casts his or her net for defendants. Lawyers for plaintiffs in these kinds of lawsuits perceive associations as deep pockets, given their ability to assess members to cover things like judgments against them. That assessment stream can work against an association.

However, do not think it is easy—or cheap—to sue. Getting someone else to take responsibility for issues that arise with the purchase of a condo requires money, perseverance, and accuracy in legal theories.

Is there any way out?

Obviously, selling your condominium is the cleanest way out, if that is the way you want to go. But selling a condo is not like leaving an apartment; there is a lot to think about. Do you have other options? Can you afford to lease it out if you do not like the living conditions? Can you cover your mortgage if you rent out the place? Are there limitations in the association's rules on renting your condo?

> **Key Point**
>
> When a purchaser becomes unhappy with a transaction, he or she may look to someone to pay. This could mean a lawsuit.

Living in a condominium shares many of the same characteristics as apartment living, but the biggest problem for condo owners is that if an owner gets into a fight with his or her neighbors, gets into an untenable living situation, or decides that the board is unresponsive, he or she cannot just call a moving truck and move on. There is a sale of one home involved and the finding and purchase of another, or finding alternative housing arrangements. There is the consideration of whether that person is sacrificing his or her life's biggest investment.

The board told me to just sell my condo if I do not like living in my association, but I do not really see that as being an option. What can I do?

No one wants to hear, "If you do not like it, sell your condo." But that is the first thing that seems to spill from the mouth of board members or neighbors with whom a dispute has developed. Being able to purchase a condominium may be a dream come true, but for some, the dream turns into a nightmare, especially when they see no way out. And there could be many reasons why selling the condo is not an option, or should be the last one. But before deciding your life is over, consider a few possible options.

- First, do everything you can do to "soothe the savage beast." Perhaps reading a book on dealing with difficult people will help, or taking a class on communications. Perhaps you could talk to someone who has knowledge or special dispensations, or a tendency to think in a balanced way; perhaps enlisting someone to role play with to help you visualize a good scenario and how to get there would be a good choice. It may sound trite, but *many* disputes arise simply from a lack of being able to communicate effectively with peers, authority figures, or difficult people.

- People can educate themselves to the extent that they know more than the people they are fighting with about the subject that is the center of the dispute. For example, if the dispute is with the board or a neighbor, a homeowner can educate him- or herself about the state law related to condo or neighborhood issues; the regulations on the property (there are many board members who are not familiar with the regulations on the property they are managing as a board); or the products or services available if the dispute involves something that could be resolved, were the resources made available to the people on the opposing side of the argument.

- Next, you might seek the help of a neutral party, a facilitator, mediator, or someone else who can assess the situation objectively and see if there are any solutions short of moving out. Understand that whatever is happening, whether it is related to a dispute with neighbors or the board, may look different to an objective observer, a person without a stake in the dispute, and especially a person who has some training in assisting people with disputes or facilitating resolutions between parties. See what this person suggests. Maybe there are solutions, but the parties are too blinded by emotions to see them.

- Consider renting out the unit and moving on, either to an apartment or another home, and see if the same problems persist. Sometimes people just simply cannot get along, but sometimes they can recognize their own flaws if the people they are fighting with can get along with others. And sometimes the need to move on becomes the catalyst to move up.

- Before giving up, seek the help of an attorney if the differences of opinion relate to legal issues. There may be a solution with a simple letter, pointing out to the neighbor or board that there is a law, or a legal solution, if the conduct continues.

What other resources can I use to educate myself on condo ownership?

You are almost there! If you read this entire book, you have educated yourself about many things related to condominium living. To further your education, you need only look as far as your computer, local library, state and other locality websites, and bookstores. There are some things to watch out for, however.

When searching for homeowners' association education on the Web, keep in mind that the words you use are important. For example, if you do a search for "homeowners association," the first many sites you will see listed on the page will probably be news sources—the media loves a good condominium horror story. On the other hand, if you do a search for "HOA law," "HOA resources," or "HOA education," you will most likely find informational sites about the area it is you are interested in learning about.

Our board hired a manager who is terrible. We are a small association and could not afford the hire in the first place. We do not want an outside manager. What are our rights as homeowners?

A homeowners' association that operates on a self-managed basis may *think* it is doing okay without professional management, but unless the board members educate themselves as to the acceptable standards of management practices and administration in their jurisdiction and have some strong financial and leadership qualities, they have a difficult chance of succeeding in the long term. The training includes educating themselves on the operations, administration, financial, and legal requirements of an association. It involves understanding the need for good communication skills and a plan for implementing them. Undergoing training may mean attending seminars regularly to keep up on current homeowners' association issues—in other words, education and continuing education. Many self-managed associations operate perfectly fine for years, but at some point end up with documents that can no longer be enforced (because neighbors have avoided enforcing the rules against other neighbors), a giant special assessment, or disastrous financial results because of mismanagement. Sometimes self-managed boards can do a better job, but usually only if the members are trained.

We do not like the manager our board hired at all, and have told the board on numerous occasions. The board refuses to act—do we have any rights?

The board chooses the management. Sometimes the regulatory documents give the owners the right to approve management, but usually the authority rests with the board. Some boards will include owners on a committee to search for management candidates, but this is not generally required.

One area where board members fall short is in the failure to adopt policies that provide for the periodic evaluation of management, or that provide for owner input or surveys about how owners feel about management. When boards are diligent about these things, it alleviates trust issues and other concerns that owners have about management. In addition, if managers know about areas where owners have concerns, in some cases the manager can make an effort to change things that might alleviate owners' concerns. It makes for a better working relationship to have periodic evaluations and give staff and contractors the opportunity to do what they can to improve relations. Accountability of managers—and other vendors, for that matter—is of the utmost importance.

We have an owner who is perfectly willing to do the books and manage the association for $200 per

month—can we use that person?

A board that ignores the value of trained, experienced, and educated management is missing the boat and jeopardizing the association's viability. If an association cannot afford professional management, then it is critical to choose a person who is willing to do the work of getting trained to do the job *right.* A lot of people assume that it is just a matter of collecting the assessments, paying the bills, and meeting once a month, but it is much more than that.

One way of looking at it is that an association cannot afford *not* to use professional management. A board that ignores the training and education standards for homeowners' association managers may be headed for personal risks and liability. Seeking out and listening to the right kinds of experts is a good faith component of service. Listening to the owners who are complaining about costs and allowing it to dictate the decision of whether to hire a trained manager is not the right thing to do. Individual owners seldom fully understand what is involved in running a homeowners' association.

Where can I look for a trained and experienced manager?

Advertising in the local newspaper is generally not the way to find a trained and experienced homeowners' association manager. Advertising in a CID industry journal or checking with groups such as those listed in the resource list published in Appendix A would be good ways to find a manager. Checking the references of the applicants for a manager position is as important as it is with any other vendor or staff person. Educating yourself by reading industry journals and articles, attending seminars, or networking with other associations that have been successful in finding good managers are other ways to locate the right kind of people. When you go to seminars, ask questions, talk to other owners, and talk to the vendors themselves.

Where can condo owners find the right kind of legal help?

Finding competent counsel to get good legal advice about an association's legal quandary is also not always easy. Again, do not put an ad in the newspaper, and beware of general practitioners, non-HOA attorneys, and even real estate attorneys if they do not have homeowners' association experience.

Many attorneys believe they are equipped to address legal questions, no matter what the specific issue. Research is available on almost any subject. However, anyone who relies on a family lawyer, probate attorney, or non-specific counsel for advice related to a condominium problem may find him- or herself in a real predicament. The reason is that condominium law is a specialty area for which there are specific laws, cases, and regulations that one needs to know for any involved legal issue. Experience may be one of the best teachers in this field of law; it definitely helps with perspective in resolving disputes between the board and a homeowner, or a homeowner and a neighbor, if you can find someone who has helped people on both sides of the issue.

Although there are many attorneys in the United States who are knowledgeable about association law, those who will accept homeowner clients are most likely in the minority. There are practical reasons why many attorneys do not accept condo owner clients. It is not easy for homeowners to bear the expense of hiring an attorney, especially when a homeowner is overburdened and tough decisions need to be made about going forward. This strain can affect the attorney/client relationship, and sometimes takes its toll on both parties.

However, owners have valid claims too. There are boards that are either ignorant of or choose to ignore the law, a practice that is much too widespread to allow the mindset that the board is always right. And owners deserve knowledgeable and capable representation as well as the boards. It does not do anybody any good when an owner hires an attorney who does not know much about homeowners' association law. If the attorney misrepresents his or her knowledge and understanding of the law, it can lead to wasteful proceedings, improper advice, and delays in resolution; be a detriment to the owner's case; and lead to a multitude of other problems for all parties. This is true, of course, in any case where an attorney does not fully understand the area in which he or she is practicing, but claims to be well-versed. Attorneys can say all kinds of things that make themselves sound smart, but advising clients in an area of the law where they have little or no expertise can lead to a malpractice claim.

Since there is such a lack of basic education in this area of real property ownership, many owners who think they have a world-winning case do not. Sometimes after learning that a case is not going as well as projected, the owners are unhappy to the point that they will look for an attorney to further their own cause, at whatever cost.

It can be a frustrating experience to look for an association attorney. One suggestion is to start with a directory from an industry group that serves your region of the country (see Appendix A), and start calling the attorneys and asking if they represent owners. If you are a homeowner, you can search out homeowner advocacy groups and see if they lead you to competent counsel. Some of the groups are pretty negative in their approach, but that will be evident to you in the group's published materials if you find any. Board members and owners alike can join some of the groups mentioned in Appendix A.

Conclusion

Hopefully, this book has offered some helpful insight as to the workings of the average condominium association. It is not as easy as it should be to gather helpful information on problem solving. However, please be sure to check out the resources listed in Appendix A—you may find helpful information there.

In addition, some states have oversight groups that homeowners or board members can go to for information and help in resolving disputes. In the future, expect states to be pushing board member education and other measures that will encourage the volunteers who serve on the boards of the associations to get more education, requirements that will most likely be followed by more educational offerings.

Glossary

A

air space. *See* unit.

articles of incorporation. A charter document filed with the state that creates corporate status for a common interest development or homeowners' association.

assessments. Money collected from the condominium owners by the association to take care of costs associated with the upkeep and repair of common-area parts of the association.

B

board of directors. The elected, deliberative body responsible for managing, planning, and setting the policy and operations of a homeowners' association or common interest development.

bylaws. An organizational document that sets up the structure of and guides the board of directors in operating the corporation.

C

community apartment project. A common interest development in which an undivided interest in land is coupled with the right of exclusive occupancy of any apartment located on the property.

common area. The entire common interest development except for separate interests.

common interest development (CID). A community apartment project, condominium project, planned development, or stock cooperative that shares some amenities.

condominium. An undivided interest in a common area within a complex, coupled with a separate interest in a space called a unit.

condominium plan. A plan that describes the physical characteristics of a condominium project.

condominium project. A development consisting of condominiums.

covenant. *See* deed restrictions.

Covenants, Conditions, and Restrictions (CC&Rs). Sometimes called the *declaration*. The key governing document for common interest developments that describes restrictions on how land may be used.

D
declaration. *See* Covenants, Conditions, and Restrictions (CC&Rs).

deed restrictions. Also *enabling declaration* or *covenant*. The documents that contain the recorded restrictions on a property.

developer. The person or group that signs and records the original declaration establishing a condominium development and the restrictions that regulate it.

director. An individual member of the board of directors. In most cases, a director is an uncompensated homeowner volunteer who is elected by vote of the association membership.

E

enabling declaration. *See* deed restrictions.

exclusive use common areas. Also *restricted use common areas.* A portion of the common area that is designated for the exclusive use of one or more, but fewer than all, of the owners of separate interests. May be designated in the CC&Rs. Specific, exclusive use common areas are identified by law.

F

fiduciary duty. A duty of trust depending on public confidence. Practically, it is the duty of a director to consider the best interests of the entire association when making corporate decisions. The duty includes an obligation to put self-interest aside if it conflicts with the best interests of the association.

G

governing documents. Also *regulatory documents.* The declaration and other documents such as bylaws, articles of incorporation, and CC&Rs, which contain rules that govern the operation of the association.

H

homeowners' association (HOA). A nonprofit corporation, usually elected, that is created for the purpose of managing a common interest development.

M

member. A person entitled to membership in an association, usually by virtue of ownership of a separate interest.

N

no partition clause. *See* nonseverability.

nonseverability. Also *no partition clause.* A clause in the declaration of a common interest development that prevents a member from separating his or her interest in the common area from that of the rest of the membership.

O

owner. The owner on title in the county recorder's official records of a separate interest or condominium. Each owner usually automatically becomes a member of the association by virtue of ownership in a separate interest or condominium.

P

planned unit development (PUD). A development in which the owners own separate lots rather than sharing ownership with others. In PUDs, the association usually owns the common area, which may consist of pools, clubhouses, greenbelt areas, parks, streets, and landscaped areas.

pro forma. An item or document provided in advance in a prescribed form. Associations must provide a pro forma budget to the membership each year in advance of the start of the fiscal year.

R

regulatory documents. *See* governing documents.

restricted use common areas. *See* exclusive use common areas.

rules. The association document that is normally prepared at the direction of the board of directors, which serves as a common reference for members of the common interest development and reflects to what official policy owners are subject. Sometimes owners are allowed to vote on the adoption of rules.

S

separate interest. The real property interest owned by an individual. In a *community apartment project*, the interest is the exclusive right to occupy an apartment. In a *condominium project*, the interest is the exclusive right to occupy an individual unit (the interior airspace) plus the ownership as a tenant-in-common with others, usually of the building. In a *planned unit development*, the interest is the exclusive right to occupy a separately owned lot, parcel, area, or space. In a *stock cooperative*, the interest is the exclusive right to occupy a portion of the real property.

stock cooperative. A common interest development in which a corporation is formed to hold title in a property, and the corporation is owned by shareholders who have a right to occupy a portion of the real property.

T

tenants-in-common. Partners in ownership of property.

townhouse. A style of housing structure that has common walls.

U

unit. The separate interest in a condominium project. This is the residential, exclusive-use area often referred to as the *air space* within the building that is owned by the individual member.

Appendix A | RESEARCHING RESOURCES

The following sections are intended to help you in finding the resources you need to learn more about condominium law.

Researching on the Internet
Do a search for your state's official government homepage by typing the name of your state in the search engine. The links to state government sites are usually formatted with the state name, followed by a period and the abbreviation "gov," e.g. **www.ohio.gov**. If you do a search simply for your state's name, the link to the government page should come up in the first few entries. Once you are at your state's home page, look for a link to state "laws," "statutes," "codes," or "legislation."

You can also do a more direct search by typing both the name of your state and the term you are trying to find information from, e.g., "Michigan legislature," which in most cases will take you directly to the state's legislation page.

Once you get to your state's legislation page, you can do a further search for information on homeowners' association law by typing in search terms like "condominium," "homeowners association," etc., which should pull up laws related to these entities. You can refine your search even further by typing a term you are interested in finding information on along with the original search term in the search engine, e.g., "condominium assessments." It also might broaden your search if you separate the two terms with the word "and," as in "condominium and assessments."

If you are looking for general information on homeowners' association law, you might try **www.communityassociations.net**, which includes state-specific information as well.

Finding Specific Publications and Other News Sources
If you are looking on the Internet for newspaper articles about homeowners' associations or condominiums, you can either search by subject, or search for state or regional newspapers and then do a search by subject within the newspaper of choice. You can also search for publications on homeowners' associations or condominiums by using a key term plus the word "articles" or "publications" in the search box.

- **Search by an author or expert**. This should be simple—to search for publications by a certain author or expert, just enter the person's name in the search engine. You may have heard of someone, e.g., an attorney, a professor, an author, or a legislator, who champions your cause. Searching by a name can bring up all kinds of information about an author and his or her publications, but be careful because there may be similar names to the one you are searching on that will bring up information that may be irrelevant to what you are researching. For example, if you type "Beth A. Grimm," into the search engine, several sites come up—my website (**www.californiacondoguru.com**), links to articles I have written, my blog (**www.communityassociations.net/cacondoguru**), my photography site, and references to other books I have written. If you scroll through to the third page of results, however, you will find references to sites about "Mary Beth Grimm." You will also most likely come across a website somewhere in the first page of listings that purports to cater to condominium and homeowners' association members that is quite anti-CAI (Community Associations Institute). Clicking into this group's site will not take you to what I would consider a credible source of information about me, but rather information flavored by this colorful group's own perspectives on CAI, life in a homeowners' association, and how bad it can be. This is an example of what can happen if a website references someone's name enough times on its site—it can piggyback on the person's work or notoriety, and the potentially misleading site will come up when the person's name is plugged into the Web search.

Be wary when searching for reputable websites. You should pay careful attention to the following items whenever you do research on the Internet, but especially when searching for information on condominiums or homeowners' associations.

- **Groups and mailing lists.** Be careful about going on to websites that require you to register your personal information before allowing you full access. Sometimes the people who collect your information distribute it or abuse it in some other way. Make sure the site offers enough information for you to determine whether you want to be put in its database. Keep in mind that identity theft is a scary reality, and be sure to take the proper precautions (i.e., read disclaimers, check to make sure contact information is provided and is accurate, etc.) before subscribing to be on any type of website database or list.

- **Negative websites.** Some of the sites that direct their services toward unhappy condo owners go to extremes in their methods, and, because of their negativity, are a source of unrest in homeowners' associations. Some sites focus on formalized, structured, and organized complaints, while others focus their wrath on industry organizations and the professionals who serve them. While some of the arguments might be legitimate, the majority most likely result from painful experiences. There are some organizations' sites that serve owners very well, however, but you need to sift through all the sites to find one that has reliable information.

- **Finding balanced information.** Websites have to have some kind of balance to be credible. The most informational sites do not tend to engage in unbridled negativity or feverish sales pitches. Bias is not usually well-disguised; look for information, as opposed to an emphasis on advertisement, if you are trying to learn about rights, responsibilities, laws, practical issues and solutions, etc. If you find yourself on a site that engages in negativity or heavy advertising, you can do one of two things: (1) leave, or (2) review the information with a filtered view. If there is a contact link, you can ask questions to help you determine the validity of the site's information, e.g., "What is the professional background of the person whom you cited as your source for [fact]?"

Tips on Web Searches

The following terms are good ones to start your condominium and homeowners' association information search.

- **Condominium.** Doing a search using this word alone will give you a host of real estate sites with condos for sale, vacation condos, etc. This is a great way to begin your search if you are looking for a condo to buy.

- **Condominium law.** Entering this term will pull up about ten pages of sites with information about various state laws, attorneys, real estate agents, and vendor sites like "Just Ask a Question" discussed later.

  You can refine the search by making it state specific or adding words like "education," "classes," "publications," "cases," "articles," etc.

- **Homeowners' associations.** Searching for this word will turn up sites that claim to be information sources or news sources, and many articles about homeowners' associations. Be sure to pay attention to the amount of negativity, bias, and overall credibility of these sites, as previously discussed, because the sources pulled up on a "homeowners' association" search can be especially tricky. One such source called Wikipedia would seem to be a source of considerable information about homeowners' associations, but as of the time of this book's publication, it was tagged with the following disclaimer: "The neutrality of this article is disputed. Please see the discussion on the talk page. Please do not remove this message until the dispute is resolved." There are also links within the disclaimer boxes that allow people to "improve" the article, i.e., add, change, or delete text to the Wikipedia entry. The "improvements" can be made by anyone, and after they have been made, they can be saved to the site and become part of the original entry.

Other Components of a Search

It can be confusing to know where to go once your search pulls up pages and pages of hits. When you do a search on "HOA law," for example, the first page that comes up might suggest you try related words with provided links, and will probably have a separate section of links labeled as "Sponsored links." Sponsored links are those that pay to advertise. One you might come across when searching "HOA law," for example, is that of the law firm Glazer and Associates, PA. Most of the page is one big advertisement, with small links to the company's blog and publications, which are informational, but short. There is a huge emphasis on advertisement for the firm, which is typical of law sites. The links to the attorney profiles, however, tend to have good information.

- **Sponsored site.** If you want to be granted full access to certain sponser sites, you have to register and create a password. Take HOATalk.com (**www.hoatalk.com**), another site listed as a sponsored site for "HOA law." Clicking into and joining this site will give you access to discussions that involve condominium and homeowners' association issues, posed mostly by board members. The purpose and intent of the site is to bring board members and others together to discuss problems and solutions. If you want to be in on a national discussion group, this is a good site for that. Just keep in mind that the solutions offered by board members and others that are based on state law are not always described as state specific, and the solution or answer may not be exactly pertinent to your state.

  You might also have to pay to get information you want from sponsored sites. At a vendor site called Just Answer (**http://law.justanswer.com**), for example, you can ask a question and get an answer from a "legal expert" for a minimal sum of money. Without speaking specifically to this site's offerings, you should know that the downside to seeking an answer to what seems like a simple question, especially a legal question, via the Internet without establishing a client/vendor relationship, is that the answer may be faulty, especially if the question is filtered in such a way that it does not reflect all the information that may pertain to it. You have to be careful of this practice, whether you are the person asking or the vendor answering the question.

- **Unsponsored sites.** These are sites that come up and are prioritized on the page based on such criteria as number of hits, freshness of content, accuracy of the term entered in the search engine, etc. Unsponsored sites are generally preferable to sponsored sites, simply because of the level of information unsponsored sites have in comparison to sponsored sites, even though the validity of some of the sites' information may be questionable.

  You should definitely search for and pay attention to state-specific information. But do not assume that all the information on any one site is completely state-specific, even if it claims to be. For example, my blog covers many practical as well as legal issues, and while these issues may be specific to California, keep in mind that California is a leader in new legislation and has a reputation for prolific legislators, so chances are some of the information might apply to your state someday if it does not already.

  Some of the other states with prolific legislative bodies of law are Florida, Hawaii, Arizona, Texas, New Jersey, and New York. Many states have adopted various forms of uniform laws such as the *Uniform Common Intrest Ownership Act* (UCIOA). California is in the process of possibly rewriting the entire body of law regulating common interest developments currently called the *Davis Stirling Common Interest Development Act*, named after the two legislators who originally authored the body of law. This is a good example of where checking the legislation in your state, or in this case, the California Law Revision Commission site, would help you know what is proposed as new law.

What follows in the next appendix are several miscellaneous links. Knowing the information presented in this appendix, you can review them and after a while, you will get a feel for what is worth pursuing further, to get what you want.

Appendix B NATIONAL AND INTERNATIONAL SITES

The following is a list of websites that offer general information about condominiums and homeowners' associations.

- **Community Associations Network**
  www.communityassociations.net
  This site provides valuable information about homeowners' associations and their issues all around the country. You will find blogs, articles, newsletters, newsfeeds, and much more.

- **Community Associations Institute (CAI)**
  www.caionline.org
  This is a national organization, with at least one chapter in each state. The state chapters and their web addresses can be located by visiting the national site and clicking on "Find a Chapter" under the link "Chapters & Affiliates." This organization offers information on educational courses, a myriad of informational resources, excellent publications, management training and certification, seminars, trade show and advertising opportunities, and legislative activities all over the country and on the federal level. The members include homeowners, board members, managers, developers, and various vendors and professionals. There is a membership fee to join CAI, and it charges a small fee for most of the publications.

Many of the programs put on by the local CAI chapters also charge only a nominal fee.

- **Robert McConnell—HOA Parliamentarian**
  www.parli.com
  Check out the information that is available on this site relating to Robert's Rules and parliamentary procedure— answers to important questions and solutions to difficult problems using Robert's Rules are a valuable part of this website, not to mention the various training publications that are available.

- **National Association of Housing Cooperatives (NAHC)**
  www.coophousing.org/member_associations.shtml
  This is a group of housing cooperatives in each state. The cooperatives and professionals are encouraged to join the NAHC through a state or city member association. Many of the member associations also accept mutual housing associations, condos, and other forms of resident-controlled housing. The benefits of joining through a member association include additional information and training, and the opportunity to be involved at a local or regional level.

- **The Canadian Condominium Institute (CCI)**
  www.cci.ca
  This is an independent, nonprofit organization that serves as a central clearinghouse on condominium issues and activities across Canada. CCI is represented provincially by local chapters and assists members in establishing and operating successful condominium corporations through education, information dissemination, workshops, and technical assistance. CCI provides objective

research for practitioners and government agencies regarding all aspects of condominium operations. Various interest groups are represented within CCI.

- **Pacific Condominium Association of British Columbia**
  www.condohelp.org
  This organization seeks to improve the lives of condominium dwellers in British Columbia through programs designed to develop education, communication, cooperation, and understanding among its member strata corporations (i.e., condominium associations).

The following are several state-specific websites that provide information on condominiums or homeowners' associations and their boards.

- **California**
  www.cidregistry.com/link2.htm
  www.hoayellowpages.com (directory of providers)

- **Florida**
  www.sunshinelist.com/2007Q2-directories.html
  www.cocafl.org/a005.html
  www.ccfj.net/HOAFLorganizations.html
  www.flsenate.gov/statutes/index.cfm?App_mode=Display_Statute&URL=Ch0720/ch0720.htm

- **Hawaii**
  www.atlist.org/condominium_association/hawaii_5.aspx
  www.mauicondocouncil.com

- **New York**
  www.fnyhc.org
  www.oag.state.ny.us/realestate/home_prob.html

- **Virginia**
  www.arlingtonva.us/DEPARTMENTS/CountyBoard/org/
  condo.asp
  www.dpor.virginia.gov/dporweb/cic_lias.cfm

Index

About the Author

Beth A. Grimm is a recognized authority on community Association law who calls upon many years experience in dealing with the problems of homeowners, board members and homeowner associations. An accomplished writer, she offers a plain English explanation of the rigths and responsibilities that come with condo living. She has been active in legislation for more than 20 years and serves as a volunteer speaker and writer for many community association industry groups and real estate groups. She has served as regional chairperson for resource groups CAI and ECHO.